AF608175

THE CATHOLIC UNIVERSITY OF AMERICA
CANON LAW STUDIES
No. 217

The Privileges of Cardinals

COMMENTARY WITH HISTORICAL NOTES

BY THE
REV. HARRY G. HYNES, S.T.L., J.C.L.
Priest of the Archdiocese of Philadelphia

A DISSERTATION

Submitted to the Faculty of the School of Canon Law of the Catholic University of America in Partial Fulfillment of the Requirements for the Degree of
DOCTOR OF CANON LAW

THE CATHOLIC UNIVERSITY OF AMERICA PRESS
WASHINGTON, D. C.
1945

Nihil Obstat:

LUDOVICUS MOTRY, S.T.D., J.C.D.,
Censor Deputatus.
Washingtonii, D. C., die 16 maii, 1945.

Imprimatur:

✠ D. CARD. DOUGHERTY,
Archiepiscopus Philadelphiensis.
Philadelphiae, die 18 maii, 1945.

Printed by
THE PAULIST PRESS
401 WEST 59TH STREET
NEW YORK 19, N. Y
51

TO MY

MOTHER, FATHER

AND SISTERS

TABLE OF CONTENTS

CHAPTER VII

CHAPTER VIII

CHAPTER IX

INTRODUCTION

Next to the Sovereign Pontiff himself, there is no office of greater dignity in the Catholic Church than that of the cardinalate. As Members of the Senate and as the principal counsellors of the Pope, it is the sublime duty of the cardinals to assist the supreme pontiff in guiding and directing the affairs of the Church universal. In the words of Pope Eugene IV, "as the door of a house turns on its hinges, so on the cardinalate does the Apostolic See, the door of the whole Church, rest and find support."[1] It is only fitting, then, that as a recompense for their many responsible duties and as an attestation of their eminent dignity in the Church, cardinals should enjoy privileges more ample and extensive than those enjoyed by any other ecclesiastics. In the years prior to the Code many such privileges were accorded to cardinals; some by express grant of the common law, others by virtue of the custom of the Roman Curia. But, at no time in history has the cardinalate been graced with such a multiplex variety of common law privileges as those so graciously conceded by the legislator of the Code of Canon Law.

Since the promulgation of the Code of Canon Law, few authors have endeavored to present a complete canonical treatment of the cardinalitial privileges contained in the Code. In the greater majority of commentaries these privileges are merely noted in passing, without further comment. Because of this lack of direct commentary, the present historico-canonical treatment of the cardinalitial privileges was undertaken. In doing so, the author has restricted himself to the individually personal privileges that have been conceded by the common law of the Code. Consequently, one of the more prominent privileges of cardinals, that of electing the new pontiff when the Apostolic See has become vacant by the death of the Pope, is not within the direct scope of this work, as it is a

[1] Const. *"Non mediocri"* (a. 1439), 14—*Codicis Iuris Canonici Fontes cura Emi. Petri Card. Gasparri editi* (Romae, postea Civitate Vaticana: Typis Polyglottis Vaticanis, 1923-1938), n. 50. (Henceforth cited as *Fontes.*)

privilege which must be exercised by the cardinals as a collegiate body.

Moreover, particular and private privileges that have been granted to cardinals who hold particular offices either within the Cardinal College or elsewhere, are outside the scope of this study. Only those privileges that have been conceded by common law and which all cardinals may make use of as individual members of the College are directly dealt with in the present dissertation. Apropos of these latter privileges, it is to be remembered that they are equally enjoyed by all cardinals *as cardinals*. The fact that a cardinal is a residential bishop who has been elevated to the cardinalate is of no added consequence. All cardinals, even those who are not endowed with the episcopal character, from the moment of their consistorial promotion, share in and enjoy these privileges in an equal degree.

Further, the author has not attempted to explore the disputed question of the precise origin of the cardinalate, nor its development through the later years of the Middle Ages. Such a work, based on the most modern research, is now in preparation by Dr. Stephen Kuttner, Professor of Canon Law History at the Catholic University of America.

The author takes this occasion to express his gratitude to His Eminence, Dennis Cardinal Dougherty, Archbishop of Philadelphia, for the opportunity of advanced study; to the Faculty of the School of Canon Law; and to all others who in any way contributed by interest and aid towards the completion of this dissertation.

CHAPTER I

PRELIMINARY REMARKS ON PRIVILEGES AND CARDINALS

ARTICLE I. THE NOTION OF PRIVILEGE

A PRIVILEGE may be defined as a concession of some special right made by a legitimate superior.[1] Privilege always denotes a relationship with law, and in the majority of cases it signifies an exemption from a law. As such, it may be conceded through a particular indult, through a law or finally *vivae vocis oraculo*. A privilege granted through a particular indult would be one granted by a rescript, as for instance, the privilege of using a portable altar. The privileges of cardinals are examples of privileges granted *per modum legis*. They are real privileges for they grant exemptions from specific regulations of the common law. They are also laws since they form part of the current legislation, that is, as privileges they have been incorporated into the common law of the Code.[2] They can therefore be referred to as *privilegia legis*.

The writer here desires to explain the use of some terminology that might otherwise give rise to confusion. The terms in question are those of strict sense and wide sense with regard to privileges. Some authors[3] refer to privileges that exist outside the Code as

[1] Roelker, *Principles of Privilege According to the Code of Canon Law*, The Catholic University of America Canon Law Studies, n. 35 (Washington, D. C., The Catholic University of America, 1926), p. 16, hereafter cited *Principles of Privilege*.

[2] Cf. *Codex Iuris Canonici Pii X Pontificis Maximi Iussu digestus Benedicti XV auctoritate promulgatus* (Romae: Typis Polyglottis Vaticanis, 1917), canons 239, § 1; 223, § 1, n. 1; 600, § 3; 604; 728, § 3; 811, § 2; 812; 1155, § 1; 1189; 1401; 1557, § 1; 1770, § 2; 2227, § 2.

[3] E. g., D'Annibale, *Summula Theologiae Moralis* (5. ed., 3 vols., Romae, 1908), I, n. 297; Cocchi, *Commentarium in Codicem Iuris Canonici* (5 vols. in 8, Taurinorum Augustae: Marietti, 1932-1940), I (5. ed. recognita, 1938), n. 161, hereafter cited *Commentarium;* Maroto, *Institutiones Iuris Canonici*

privileges in the strict sense and refer to those contained within the Code as *privileges in the wide sense.*

The writer following Roelker [4] prefers to apply the term of *strict sense* to a privilege which the grantee is free to use or neglect, whether it be contained in the Code or exist outside the Code, and the term *wide sense* to a privilege whose use the grantee is not at liberty to neglect, whether it be a privilege contained within the Code or one that exists outside of it.

In view of the writer's terminology, cardinalitial privileges are privileges in the strict sense, since, even though they are contained within the Code, cardinals are free to use or neglect the use of most of these privileges.[5]

In referring directly to privileges contained within the Code, the writer prefers the term *privilegia legis seu intra Codicem contenta;* while for those granted outside the Code e.g. through a particular indult, the writer prefers the term *privilegia extra Codicem concessa.*[6]

Privileges may be divided into *real* privileges, i.e., those that adhere to some dignity, place or duty, and *personal* privileges, i.e., those conceded directly in favor of a person. Personal privileges are either individually, commonly or corporately personal. An *individually personal* privilege is one granted to a physical person. A *commonly personal* privilege is one granted to a physical person because he belongs to a certain state or possesses a certain dignity. A *corporately personal* privilege is one conceded to a moral person, as for example, to a community or religious order. The privileges of cardinals as contained in the Code of Canon Law are commonly personal privileges.[7]

(2 vols., Romae, Matriti, 1919-1921), I (Romae, 1921), n. 291-292; Cicognani, *Canon Law* (authorized English version by Rev. Joseph M. O'Hara and Rev. Francis Brennan, Philadelphia: Dolphin Press, 1935), pp. 779-781.

[4] *Principles of Privilege,* pp. 7-8.

[5] The writer would refer to the clerical privileges contained in canons 119, 120, 121 and 122 as privileges in the *wide sense,* since, even though they are contained within the Code, the use of such privileges may not be surrendered.

[6] Cf. canon 71. A full treatment of *privilegia intra et extra Codicem* is contained in an article by Rudolf Köstler, "Der Aufbau des katholischen Kirchenrechts. Ein Beitrag zur theorie seiner Quellen"—*Zeitschrift für oeffentliches Recht* (Wien und Berlin, 1919/1920—), Bd. VI (Springer, 1922), 479-487.

[7] Cf. Roelker, *op. cit.*, pp. 31-32; Cicognani, *op. cit.*, pp. 781-782.

Once the cardinalitial dignity has been conferred upon him, a cardinal cannot renounce his privileges.[8] Nor, since these privileges partake of the nature of laws, can they be renounced by the cardinals as a body.[9] To revoke them a new general law is required.[10] Finally, since the privileges of cardinals are commonly and not individually personal privileges, they do not cease with the death of the prelate. They must, however, be considered personal at least in the sense that their use is legitimate wherever the grantee happens to be.[11]

It should be further noted that since cardinals are comprehended under the term *cleric* when it involves a *materia non odiosa*,[12] they share in the privileges accorded to clerics by the common law.[13] That cardinals had to be clerics was decreed by Sixtus V (1585-1590) in his famous constitution on the cardinalate wherein he stated that no one was to be raised to the cardinalate unless he had been tonsured and in Minor Orders for at least one year and that anyone nominated as a cardinal deacon had to receive the diaconate, if lacking it, within one year of his nomination.[14] Today, the requirement is even more extensive as the Code stipulates that to be elevated to the cardinalate one must of necessity be at least a priest.[15]

Moreover, as will be seen in the treatment of the individual privileges, many of the cardinalitial privileges as enumerated in the Code are also episcopal privileges in which the cardinals, even though

[8] Canon 72, § 3: *Concesso alicui communitati, dignitati locove renuntiare privatis personis non licet.*

[9] Canon 72, § 4: *Nec ipsi communitati seu coetui integrum est renuntiare privilegio sibi dato per modum legis. . . .*

[10] Canon 71: *Per legem generalem revocantur privilegia in hoc codice contenta. . . .*

[11] Canon 74: *Privilegium personale personam sequitur et cum ipsa exstinguitur. Nota*: The use of some of the cardinalitial privileges is prohibited in the city of Rome and in certain other specific instances. These will be noted in the treatment of the individual privileges.

[12] Cf. Diana, *Resolutiones Morales* (ed. novissima, 10 tomi in 5 vols., Venetiis, 1728), vol. 5, tom. 9, tract. 7: *De Potestate et Privilegiis S.R.E. Cardinalium*, res. 68.

[13] Cf. canons 119, 120, 121 and 122.

[14] Const. *Postquam*, 3 dec. 1586, §§ 6, 15—*Fontes*, n. 159.

[15] Canon 232, § 1.

not bishops, came to share because of their exalted position in the administration of ecclesiastical affairs.[16]

ARTICLE II. THE DIGNITY OF THE CARDINALATE

Next to the Roman Pontiff there is in the Catholic Church no ecclesiastical dignity higher than that of the cardinalate. Whatever may be said of the origin of the cardinalate, it is beyond dispute that during the period of ecclesiastical reform instituted by Pope Leo IX (1049-1054) the term *cardinal* began to refer to one engaged in the administration of the affairs of the universal Church. At that time the three groups of cardinals—cardinal bishops, cardinal priests and cardinal deacons—began to assist the Pope in the deliberations for the Roman Synods, which were the chief means of reform. With the inception of the twelfth century, these synods lost their force and the Pope began to hold regular assemblies with the cardinals, who were then a college or closed body. The first of these *consistories* took place under Pope Paschal II (1099-1118). The reforms enacted therein were carried out by legates, and in the majority of cases such legates were selected from the College of Cardinals.[17]

The cardinals were then definitely constituted as the senate of the Church and the principal advisors and counsellors of the Supreme Pontiff.[18]

It was with reference to this sublime duty that a later pontiff, Eugene IV (1431-1447), termed the cardinals "The hinges upon which the government of the whole Church turns." [19]

[16] The arrangement of canons 349 on the privileges of bishops and 239, § 1, on those of cardinals makes it appear that bishops share in the cardinalitial privileges while historically the converse was true. Laymann (1574-1635) in his *Theologia Moralis* (ed. nova, Venetiis, 1630), lib. I, tract. V, pars 3, c. 2, n. 2, spoke of the practice of the Church *per quam privilegia episcopis ob status dignitatem concessa, ad cardinales ferme extendi solent, propter maiorem eorum dignitatem*.

[17] Cf. Hilling, *Procedure at the Roman Curia* (translated from the German, New York, 1907), pp. 10-18, 28.

[18] Cf. canon 230: S.R.E. Cardinales Senatum Romani Pontificis constituunt eidemque in regenda Ecclesia praecipui consiliarii et adiutores assistunt.

[19] Const. *Non mediocri* (a. 1439), § 14—*Fontes*, n. 50.

Since the cardinals' relationship with the Pope was now a most intimate one, the concept of the exalted dignity of the cardinalate increased tremendously. This is apparent from many papal documents. Cardinals were said to constitute with the Pope *unum corpus* of which the Pope was the *caput* and they the *membra.*[20] They were referred to as a "part of his body, the contiguous and principal members."[21] Pope Sixtus V (1585-1590) referred to them as the "principal and most noble members of the person of the Pope."[22] Another proof of their dignity founded on this intimate relationship with the Pope is seen in the fact that they were referred to as the *inviscerati papae.*[23] When mentioning them in papal documents the pontiffs often referred to them as *fratres nostri.*[24]

Many other appellations manifest the exalted dignity of the cardinalate. By analogy drawn from Roman law they were considered as equivalent to *senatores* and *patritii.*[25] They were also likened to the *praesides,* the *proconsules* and the *prefecti praetoriani* mentioned in Roman law.[26] Besides these imperial analogies, a regal one was added insofar as they were considered the equals of princes and ceded place only to kings.[27]

[20] Cf. introductory gloss to c. 1, *de officio legati,* I, 15, in VI°.

[21] Eugene IV (1431-1447), const. *Non mediocri* (a. 1439), 6—*Fontes,* n. 50. This pope further stated that the custom of showing honor to the cardinals has been approved by the popes because honor shown the cardinals was thought to be attributed to the pope whose members they were (*ibid.,* § 10).

[22] Const. *Postquam,* 3 dec. 1586, §§ 1, 3—*Fontes,* n. 159.

[23] C. 5, *de poenis,* V, 9, in VI°.

[24] In a gloss (s. v. *fratribus nostris*) to a decree (c. 1, *de officio legati,* I, 15, in VI°) of Innocent IV (1243-1254), it was asserted that when the pope spoke promiscuously of the cardinals, i. e., when he indiscriminately referred to cardinal bishops, cardinal priests or cardinal deacons, he called them *fratres.* He also used this term when he spoke specifically of the cardinal bishops, while in referring to cardinal priests or cardinal deacons he used the term *filii.*

[25] C. 14, D.XCVI.

[26] Cf. Plati (1548-1591), *De Dignitate et Officio Cardinalis* (6. ed., cura Alexandri Card. Spada, Romae, 1836), p. 389.

[27] One of their titles of address is that of *Eminentissimi Principes.* In article 21 of the Lateran Pact (Feb. 11, 1929) it is stated that in Italy Cardinals enjoy all the honors and prerogatives that are had by the princes of the reigning royal family. Cf. *Acta Apostolicae Sedis, Commentarium Officiale*

Pope Sixtus V (1585-1590) likened the cardinals to the seventy elders who assisted Moses, and for this reason he established their number at seventy.[28]

Another evidence of this high dignity is gained from the severe punishments that were to be inflicted on anyone who made an attempt on the life of a cardinal. Such a person was declared to be just as guilty of the *crimen laesae maiestatis* as he would have been had he made the attempt on the life of the Pope.[29]

Many other statements could be adduced to illustrate the exalted position the cardinalate holds in the Church. However, it is not the intention of this work to give a detailed treatment of that topic.[30]

(Romae, 1909—), XXI (1929), 219 (hereafter cited as *AAS*); *Apollinaris* (Romae, 1928—), III (1930), 413.

[28] Const. *Postquam,* 3 dec. 1586, § 4—*Fontes,* n. 159. This was one of the reasons given by some of the earlier authors for stating that the cardinalate was of divine institution, e.g., Manfredus (sixteenth century), *De Perfecto Cardinali S.R.E. Liber* (Bononiae, 1584), pp. 2, 3; Albanus (1504-1591), *Liber de Cardinalatu* (Romae, 1541), pp. III-IV. As Wernz (1842-1914) asserts, such an opinion is today *plane improbabilis.* Cf. *Ius Decretalium* (6 vols. in 7, Romae et Prati, 1899-1913), II, n. 624.

[29] Cf. c. 5, *de poenis,* V, 9, in VI°. This was a famous decree in which Boniface VIII (1294-1303) enacted severe punishments not only against the party guilty of such a crime but also against his sons, if any, and certain relatives. Cf. also the introductory gloss to c. 1, *de officio legati,* I, 15, in VI°. This punishment was based on the Roman law wherein one who made an attempt on the life of a senator was just as guilty of the *crimen laesae maiestatis* as if he had attacked the emperor. Cf. C. (9, 8) 5. It has already been pointed out that a parallel exists between the senators of Roman law and the cardinals, hence a similar punishment. Pope Eugene IV (1431-1447) in stressing the dignity of the cardinalate referred to this punishment in his constitution *Non mediocri* (a. 1439), § 6—*Fontes,* n. 50. Pope Leo X (1513-1521) confirmed these punishments in his constitution *Supernae dispositionis,* 5 maii, 1514, § 40—*Fontes,* n. 65.

[30] For a more complete treatment of this topic the reader is referred to the following: const. *Non mediocri* (a. 1439)—*Fontes,* n. 50, in which Pope Eugene IV undertook to discuss this point in detail; Azorius, *Institutiones Morales* (3 vols.), II (Mediolani, 1617), p. 235, c. 1; Germonius (1551-1627), *De Sacrorum Immunitatibus Libri Tres* (Romae, 1591), p. 165, n. 42; Barbosa (1589-1649), *Iuris ecclesiastici universi libri III* (3 vols., Lugduni, 1650), I, c. IV; Cohellius (fl. 1623), *Notitia Cardinalatus* (Romae, 1653), pp. 16 ff.; Andreucci (1684-1771), *Hierarchia Ecclesiastica* (2 vols., Romae, 1766), diss.

Still, a brief treatment was mandatory in this work because the concept of the cardinals' dignity is fundamental to any discussion of their privileges. It is precisely because of their dignity that the many privileges they have possessed at various times were conferred upon them. Their chief duty is to assist the Pope in the government of the universal Church, a task of vast importance. It is but fitting, then, that those who are charged with such a task should enjoy many special privileges. Innocent IV (1243-1254) alluded to this in excepting cardinals from a statute which limited the power of certain legates to confer benefices. He declared that since cardinals when acting as legates enjoyed certain honorific prerogatives, he desired that they be endowed with the fullest authority for the accomplishment of their mission.[31]

Article III. General Historical Notes On Cardinalitial Privileges [32]

With regard to the historical background of the privileges of cardinals it is to be noted at the outset that many, indeed most, of the privileges that cardinals enjoyed before the Code were theirs by custom rather than by written law. This conclusion was arrived at by the writer in view of the following facts.

A. It is certain that in earlier times, i. e., during the fourteenth, fifteenth and sixteenth centuries, cardinals enjoyed many privileges. Indeed, the number of privileges then possessed far exceeded the number they enjoy since the promulgation of the Code. Ferraris

II: *De Dignitate, Officio et Privilegiis, S.R.E. Cardinalium*, pp. 21 ff.; Diana, *Resolutiones Morales*, V, tom. 9, tract. 7: *De Potestate et Privilegiis S.R.E. Cardinalium*, res. 1; Sägmüller, Lehrbuch des katholischen Kirchenrechts, I (Freiburg im Breisgau, 1925-1934), 515 ff.; Hinschius (1835-1898), *Das Kirchenrecht der Katholiken und Protestanten in Deutschland* (6 vols., Berlin, 1869-1897), Vols. I-IV: *System des katholischen Kirchenrechts* (Berlin, 1869-1888), I (Berlin, 1869), 309 ff.

31 "*. . . quod in fratribus nostris legatione fungentibus nolumus observari, quia sicut honoris praerogativa laetantur, sic eos auctoritate fungi volumus ampliori.*" Cf. c. 1, *de officio legati*, I, 15, in VI°.

32 The history of the privileges as now contained in the Code will be noted with the treatment of each individual privilege.

(+ 1763) in treating this subject set down only a few of the more important of their privileges because he feared that to enumerate them completely would exhaust his limited space. He further added that the authors of those earlier periods were by no means agreed on the exact number actually possessed by the cardinals. Albanus (Giovanni Geronimo Alboni, 1504-1591) enumerated thirty-three. Cohellius (fl. 1623) indicated forty-one. Manfredus (Girolamo Manfredi, 16th century) went as high as eighty-nine, while Germonius (Anastasio Germonius, 1551-1627) spoke of an anonymous writer who in a manuscript work set the number at three hundred.[33]

Some of the more interesting of these earlier privileges, most of which are now obsolete, were the following:

1. Before a cardinal could be convicted of a crime, seventy-two witnesses were required for a cardinal bishop, sixty-four for a cardinal priest and twenty-seven for a cardinal deacon.[34]

2. Should a schism arise from the fact that there were two contenders for the papacy, the cardinals as a body were privileged to convoke a General Council to settle the dispute.[35]

3. Cardinals had the exclusive right to judge the contentious or criminal cases of members of their households, and for punishments maintained their own private prisons.[36]

4. Cardinals enjoyed a privilege similar to that of soldiers of making a will without observing the solemnities required by law.[37]

5. Cardinals also enjoyed a multiplex variety of privileges regarding the conferral of various benefices.[38]

[33] Cf. Ferraris, *Prompta Bibliotheca, Canonica, Juridica, Moralis, Theologica, necnon Ascetica, Polemica, Rubricistica, Historica* (ed. Migne, 8 vols., Parisiis, 1860-1863), s. v. *cardinalis,* art. IV. (Hereafter cited as *Bibliotheca.*)

[34] C. 2, C. II, q. 5.

[35] Cf. Albanus, *De Cardinalatu,* quest. XLII, p. XCV; Fagnanus (1598-1678), *Commentaria in Quinque Libros Decretalium* (5 vols. in 3, Venetiis, 1696), in c. 14, X, *de maioritate et obedientia,* I, 33, n. 50 (henceforth cited as *Commentaria*); Barbosa (1589-1649), *Iuris ecclesiastici universi libri III,* I, cap. IV, n. 84.

[36] Cf. Card. Tuscus (1534-1620), *Practicae Conclusiones Iuris in omni foro Frequentiores* (9 vols., Lugduni, 1634-1670), I, C, concl. 100, n. 52, hereafter cited *Conclusiones Frequentiores.*

[37] Cf. Ferraris, *Bibliotheca,* s. v. cardinalis, art. IV.

[38] Cf. *Regulae Cancellariae Clementi XII—Bullarum Diplomatum et Privi-*

These are but a few of the many privileges enumerated by the earlier authors. The writer wishes to stress the point that these authors could not agree on the number of privileges that cardinals then actually enjoyed.

B. When one investigates the various privileges set down by these earlier authors, from a canonico-historical viewpoint it becomes apparent that there was documentary evidence in the decrees and canons of pre-Code legislation for only a few of these privileges. Still, the authors spoke of the cardinals as enjoying all of them.

C. Diana (1586-1663), who discussed cardinalitial privileges at length, in referring to one of these privileges, namely, that of being qualified to grant an indulgence of 100 days, expressly stated that the cardinals enjoyed this privilege by custom rather than by law.[39]

In view of these facts it seems justifiable to conclude that the custom of the Roman Curia and not written law constituted the historical basis of most of the privileges enjoyed by cardinals prior to the Code.

That many privileges could have arisen in this manner is understandable when one considers the interplay of two factors intimately associated with the early evolution of the cardinalate. The first was the recognition, after much dispute, of the cardinalate as a dignity higher than that of the episcopate. With the acceptance of the cardinalate as a more excellent dignity, cardinals were accorded the privilege of preceding bishops and other prelates.[40]

The second factor that gave rise to this use of privileges was the fact that in their title churches cardinals enjoyed certain rights and privileges comprehended under the general term of *quasi-episcopal*

legiorum S.R. Pontificum Taurinensis Editio (20 vols., Augustae Taurinorum, 1857-1872; 5 vols., Neapoli, 1867-1885), XXIII, 18 (henceforth cited as *Bull. Rom.*); Diana, *Resolutiones Morales, ibid.*, res. 23, sq.

[39] *Resolutiones Morales, ibid.*, res. 46. Cf. also Sägmüller, *Die Thatigkeit und Stellung der Cardinale bis Papst Bonifaz VIII* (Freiburg, 1896), p. 152, n. 11.

[40] The dignity of the cardinalate was briefly seen in the preceding article. The cardinals' right to precedence, being a privilege now contained in the Code, will be investigated historically in the treatment of the individual privileges.

jurisdiction. They were in their title churches what a bishop was in his diocese.[41]

Because of their higher dignity and right to precedence over bishops that followed from it, it seems justifiable to assume, in view of the lack of documentary evidence in pre-Code legislation, that the cardinals began to use outside their title churches, with at least the tacit consent of the Pope, many of the privileges that by law were to be used only within the title church. Then, in the course of time some of these customs were expressly ratified by the pontiffs and became privileges in the sense of written law.[42]

Prior to the promulgation of the Code only one list of cardinalitial privileges can be found among the decrees and constitutions emanating from the Holy See. On December 20, 1911, Pius X in a secret consistory with the cardinals issued a list of fifteen privileges which with others, were to be contained in the new Code under canon 239, § 1. These fifteen privileges the cardinals could make use of as of that date, six years prior to the promulgation of the Code.[43]

> I. *Audiendi ubique terrarum confessiones etiam religiosorum utriusque sexus et absolvendi ab omnibus peccatis et censuris, exceptis tantum censuris specialissimo modo Sedi Apostolicae reservatis, et illis quae adnexae sunt revelationi secreti S. Officii.*
>
> II. *Sibi suisque familiaribus eligendi sacerdotem confessionibus excipiendis, qui, si iurisdictione careat, eam ipso iure obtineat, etiam quod spectat ad peccata et censuras a quibus iidem Cardinales absolvere possunt.*
>
> III. *Celebrandi vel aliis permittendi ut coram se celebrent Missam in feria V maioris hebdomadae ac tres Missas in nocte Natalis Domini.*
>
> IV. *Sacrum celebrandi in quolibet privato sacello absque praeiudicio utentis indulto.*

[41] The rights and privileges formerly enjoyed by cardinals in their title churches will be enumerated in Article IV of this chapter.

[42] Cf. decree of Sac. Cong. of Ceremonies, 10 iun., 1630, regarding cardinals' right to use the title "*Eminentissimi.*" This decree is quoted in "*Dignité des Cardinaux*"—*Analecta Iuris Pontificii* (Romae, 1855-1869; Parisiis, 1872-1891), II (1857), 1918 sq.

[43] Cf. *Il Monitore Ecclesiastico* (Romae, 1876—), Serie III, V (1913) (Vol. XXV della interna collezione), 387.

V. *Fruendi altari privilegiato personali quotidiano; item, altari portatili, quovis decenti loco, pro eorum prudenti arbitrio, etiam in mari, servatis debitis cautelis.*

VI. *Lucrandi in propriis sacellis indulgentias, ad quas acquirendas praescripta sit visitatio templi alicuius vel publicae aediculae civitatis seu loci quo Cardinales actu commorentur; quo privilegio etiam eorum familiares frui possunt.*

VII. *Benedicendi ubique, solo crucis signo, cum omnibus indulgentiis a Sancta Sede concede solitis, rosaria, aliasque coronas precatorias, cruces, numismata, statuas, scapularia a Sede Apostolica probata, istaque imponendi absque onere inscriptionis.*

VIII. *Sub unica benedictione erigendi in ecclesiis, et oratoriis etiam privatis, in quibus missa celebrari possit, aliisque piis locis stationes Viae Crucis cum omnibus indulgentiis, quae huiusmodi exercitium peragentibus impertitae sint; nec non benedicendi pro fidelibus, qui causa infirmitatis vel alterius legitimi impedimenti sacras stationes Viae Crucis visitare nequeant, Crucifixi icones cum applicatione omnium indulgentiarum devoto exercitio eiusdem Viae Crucis a Sede Apostolica adnexarum.*

IX. *More episcoporum gestandi crucem ante pectus etiam supra mozetam ac utendi mitra et baculo pastorali.*

X. *Benedicendi ubique populo more episcoporum, sed in Urbe in ecclesiis tantum, piis locis et fidelium consessibus.*

XI. *Pontificalia cum throno et baldachino peragendi in omnibus ecclesiis, Ordinario praemonito, si ecclesia sit cathedralis; in Urbe autem ius throni non habent nisi in ecclesia sui tituli.*

XII. *Honoribus tribui solitis Ordinariis locorum fruendi quocumque se conferant.*

XIII. *Praecedendi omnes Praelatos etiam Patriarchas, imo ipsos Legatos Pontificios, nisi Legatus sit Cardinalis in proprio territorio residens; Cardinalis autem Legatus a latere praecedit omnes alios.*

XIV. *Concedendi indulgentiam ducentorum dierum in locis vel institutis ac pro personis suae iurisdictionis vel protectionis; item in aliis locis, sed a praesentibus solummodo, singulis vicibus, lucrandam.*

XV. *Consecrationes et benedictiones ecclesiarum, altarium, sacrae supellectilis, abbatum aliasve similes, excepta oleorum sacrorum consecratione, ubique, servatis servandis, peragendi.*

Ex Audientia SS.mi, die XX Decembris a MDCCCCXI.

SS.mus D. N. Pius PP. X benigne indulgere dignatus est ut S.R.E. Cardinales privilegiis quae praecedunt, etiam ante Codicis promulgationem, uti valeant.

PETRUS CARDINALIS GASPARRI.

Of the privileges in this list some were completely new while many others found in it their first expression in the form of written law.[44]

Finally, on August 20, 1917—subsequent to the promulgation of the new Code but prior to the date on which it began to oblige legally [45]—Pope Benedict XV permitted the cardinals to use from that day on the other cardinalitial privileges contained in the new Code.[46]

Article IV. Rights and Privileges Formerly Enjoyed By Cardinals In Their Title Churches and Deaconries

As has been noted it was this group of privileges reserved for use only in the cardinals' title churches, that the cardinals because of their higher dignity and precedence apparently began to use even outside their title churches. In so doing, they came to possess by custom many privileges free of local or territorial limitations.

The present law on this topic is much narrower in its extension than was that of the thirteenth century. It states that once a cardinal priest or a cardinal deacon has taken canonical possession of his title church he may perform therein the same functions that local ordinaries perform in their churches. It then greatly modifies this statement by excepting all judicial matters that might arise in that church as well as all jurisdiction over the faithful of that church.[47]

The former law up to the eighteenth century gave cardinals many jurisdictional rights and privileges. Two decrees, one of Honorius

[44] Cf. *Razon y Fe* (Madrid, 1901—), XXXIII (1912), 243-245.

[45] The Code was promulgated on May 18, 1917, and was to take legal effect on May 19, 1918.

[46] *"Beatissimus pater, in audientia die 19 mensis augusti infrascripto Cardinali data, . . . motu proprio concessit ut S.R.E. Cardinales iam nunc omnibus ac singulis fruantur privilegiis quae can. 239, § 1; 240, 600, n. 3; 1189, 1401, eiusdem codicis describuntur. Quae omnia promulgari iussit, contrariis quibuslibet minime obstantibus.*

Ex aedibus Vaticanis die 20 mensis augusti anni 1917.

R. Card. Gasparri, a Secretis Status."

Cf. *AAS*, IX (1917), 475.

[47] Cf. canon 240, § 2.

III (1216-1227) which directly concerned the rights of a cardinal over the clerics of his title church,[48] the other of Boniface VIII (1294-1303) which concerned the powers of bishops and their cathedral chapters,[49] formed the basis of this earlier law. In a gloss to the latter decree, Ioannes Andreae (1274-1348) referred to the decree of Honorius and quoted Joannes Monachus (+ 1313) as having said that Boniface VIII had given him the unqualified response that cardinals had in their title churches the same rights as bishops.[50]

Pope Paul IV (1555-1591) in speaking of the title churches of cardinals expressly stated that cardinals therein enjoyed episcopal jurisdiction.[51]

Pope Sixtus V referred to this jurisdictioneas *quasi-episcopal.*[52] By this terminology he meant to signify that since they did not have episcopal Orders, they did not have episcopal jurisdiction *qua tale.* The jurisdiction they possessed was theirs by way of privilege.

Cardinal Albitius (Albizzi) (1591-1684), in his famous work on the jurisdiction of cardinals in their title churches, thoroughly investigated the question and using the aforementioned statement of Boniface VIII as his authority concluded that cardinals, whether priests or deacons, had in their title churches the same rights that bishops had in their dioceses.[53] According to Albitius, since all

[48] C. 11, X, *de maioritate et obedientia,* I, 33.

[49] C. un., *de maioritate et obedientia,* I, 17, in VI°.

[50] Cf. marginal addition n. 3 in gloss s. v *episcopali sede,* c. 1, *de maioritate et obedientia,* I, 17, in VI°.

[51] Const. *Cum venerabilis,* 22 aug. 1555, § 1: " . . . *iidem cardinales sunt pars corporis et membra ipsius Romani Pontificis, ac diversis Almae Urbis nostrae Parochialibus Ecclesiis, pro eorum Cardinalatus titulo seu denominatione, et in eis episcopalem iurisdictionem habeant . . ."*—*Fontes,* n. 89.

[52] Const. *"Religiosa,"* 13 apr. 1587, in introductione; " . . . singulis Presbyteris, et Diaconis Cardinalibus propriae in Urbe Ecclesiae, Tituli videlicet, et Diaconiae cum suis Clero, et Populo, ac *quasi Episcopali iurisdictione* in spiritualibus, et temporalibus regendae, et administrandae committantur."—*Fontes,* n. 160.

[53] *Disceptatio de Iurisdictione quam habent S.R.E. Cardinales in Ecclesiis Titulorum,* n. 31. This work is contained in the *Theatrum Veritatis et Iustitiae* of Cardinal de Luca (1614-1683) (15 tomi in 9 vols., Coloniae-Agrippinae, 1706), IV, t. VIII, p. 220 sq.

cardinals, i. e. cardinal priests and cardinal deacons (cardinal bishops do not come under consideration here since they are actually bishops ruling over a diocese and their rights in their dioceses are necessarily those of bishops) had this quasi-episcopal jurisdiction, they had the following rights and privileges in their title churches: [54]

1. They could make laws binding in conscience.[55]

2. They had the right of correction and could impose sentences of excommunication, suspension and interdict.[56]

3. They had the right of visitation as the bishop has in his diocese.[57]

4. They had the right of conferring benefices in these churches.[58] This was to be understood as applying only when they were present in the city of Rome.[59]

5. They had the *cura animarum* of their parishioners.[60]

6. They had the right of using the pontifical insignia and of imparting the solemn blessing in the manner of a bishop, although they were not bishops themselves.[61] The cardinal deacon's right

[54] *Ibid.*, n. 43, ss. Germonius, *Tractatus de Indultis Apostolicis* (Romae, 1590), p. 24, n. 6; p. 84; Azorius, *Institutiones Morales*, II, p. 244, c. 3.

[55] Cf. Albitius, *op. cit.*, n. 43; Diana, *Resolutiones Morales*, *ibid.*, res. 40.

[56] Cf. c. 11, X, *de maioritate et obedientia*, I, 33; Fagnanus (1598-1687), *Commentaria*, in c. 11, X, *de maioritate et obedientia*, I, 33, n. 19.

[57] Council of Basle (1431-1438), sess. 23, cap. IV.—cf. Hardouin, *Acta Conciliorum et Epistolae Decretales ac Constitutiones Summorum Pontificum* (12 vols., Parisiis, 1714-1715), VIII, 1206, hereafter cited *Hardouin*. *Nota*: There is much dispute as to whether this council can legitimately be referred to as ecumenical. The true opinion, according to Schroeder (*Disciplinary Decrees of the General Councils* [St. Louis: Herder, 1937], pp. 456 ff.), seems to be that the Council of Basle was ecumenical in its first 25 sessions. This ecumenicity, however, does not cover all the decrees enacted in those sessions but only those not prejudicial to the authority of the Apostolic See. Cf. also Fagnanus, *ibid.*, n. 20.

[58] This faculty was granted by Sixtus IV according to Diana, *Resolutiones Morales*, *ibid.*, res. 52. The present law on this matter is contained in canons 1432 and 1414, § 4.

[59] Cf. Wernz, *Ius Decretalium*, II, n. 632.

[60] Council of Basle, sess. 23, cap. IV—Hardouin, VIII, 1206.

[61] Cf. Hostiensis (+1271), *Commentaria in Quinque Libros Decretalium* (6 vols. in 3, Venetiis, 1581), in c. 1, X, *de supplenda negligentia praelatorum*, I, 10, n. 5; hereafter cited *Commentaria;* Fagnanus, *Commentaria*, in c. 16, X,

in this regard was long disputed, but Albitius, after discussing both sides of the question, concluded that the cardinal deacon also shared in this right.[62] Their right was definitely established by a decree of the Sacred Congregation of Rites dated September 15, 1668.[63] It was stated therein that cardinal deacons had the right of imparting the solemn blessing in their deaconries with one exception, namely, that they could not impart it when a bishop was celebrating Mass in their title church.

7. They had the right of conferring tonsure and minor orders.[64] Sanchez (1550-1610) claimed that the Council of Trent had abrogated such faculties, since it expressly revoked any and all customs, even immemorial, if they stood contrary to its law.[65] This opinion lacked convincing force since chapter 10 of session XXIII spoke not of cardinals but expressly of abbots.[66] Even if this decree could be said to refer to cardinals, it is evident from the decree itself that the faculty of conferring tonsure and minor orders *on their subjects* i. e. those pertaining to their title churches or deaconries, was preserved.

8. They could dispense their subjects in all cases in which bishops could dispense by law.[67] This power was understood as not extending to the faculty granted to bishops by the Council of Trent to dispense from all occult irregularities, except that arising from volun-

de poenitentiis et remissionibus, V, 38, n. 42 and in c. 11, X, *de maioritate et obedientia,* I, 33, n. 24.

[62] *Op. cit.*, n. 68: *"Intrepide sentio Cardinales Diaconos habere istam potestatem in suis diaconiis, non quidem iure proprio sed ex apostolico privilegio. Cum enim in suis diaconiis habent iura episcopalia vel quasi, non est dubitandum quin stante huiusmodi privilegiis possunt solemniter benedicere."*

[63] S.R.C., *"Romana,"* 15 sept. 1668—*Fontes,* n. 5571.

[64] Cf. Albitius, *op. cit.*, n. 6; Hostiensis, *Commentaria,* in c. 1, X, *de supplenda negligentia praelatorum,* I, 10, n. 5; Fagnanus, *Commentaria,* in c. 11, X, *de maioritate et obedientia,* I, 33, n. 25.

[65] *Consilia Moralia* (2 vols. in 1, Lugduni, 1634), lib. 7, c. 1, dub. 19, n. 21.

[66] Conc. Trident., sess. XXIII, *de ref.*, cap. 10: "Abbatibus ac aliis quibuscumque quantumvis exemptis non liceat in posterum intra fines alicuius dioecesis consistentibus, etiam si nullius dioecesis vel exempti esse dicantur, cuiquam, qui regularis subditus sibi non sit, tonsuram vel minores ordines conferre." . . .—Schroeder, *Canons and Decrees of the Council of Trent,* original text with English translation (St. Louis: Herder, 1941), 442.

[67] Albitius, *op. cit.*, n. 72.

tary homicide, for this faculty was granted in contemplation of a "*dioecesis propria et plena.*" [68] Fagnanus speaking of this faculty of bishops stated that Gregory XIII (1572-1585) had asserted his unwillingness that this power should also belong to cardinals in their titles and deaconries.[69]

9. They could grant indulgences of 100 days. This power they enjoyed in virtue of custom, rather than by written grant.[70]

These in brief were the rights and privileges possessed by cardinals in their title churches by reason of their quasi-episcopal jurisdiction. These rights they retained until the time of Innocent XII (1691-1700). That pontiff transferred all jurisdiction over the clergy and the faithful of their title churches to the exclusive competence of the Cardinal Vicar of Rome, leaving to the individual cardinal priests and deacons only administrative and corrective powers.[71] They did not lose the privilege of enjoying certain honorific pontifical rights and of imparting blessings in the episcopal manner. Moreover, they still retained the right of freely conferring benefices which pertained to their title churches and deaconries.[72]

The Code has incorporated this legislation of Innocent XII so that the rights and privileges of cardinal priests and cardinal deacons in their title churches are today the same as they were under Pope Innocent XII.[73]

[68] Conc. Trident., sess. XXIV, *de ref.*, cap. 6—Schroeder, *op. cit.*, 444; cf. Albitius, *ibid.*, nn. 74, 75; Diana, *ibid.*, res. 37.

[69] *Commentaria*, in c. 11, X, *de maioritate et obedientia*, I, 33, n. 16.

[70] Albitius, *op. cit.*, n. 79; Diana, *ibid.*, res. 46.

[71] Const. "*Romanus Pontifex*," 17 sept. 1692—*Bull. Rom.*, XX, 461.

[72] Cf. Wernz, *Ius Decretalium*, II, n. 632.

[73] Cf. canons 240, § 2; 1414, § 4, and 1432, § 1, together with response of S.C.C., 12 iun. 1943—*AAS*, XXXV (1943), 399; *The Jurist* (Washington, D. C., 1941—3, IV (1944), 630-632. A recent work on this topic is: M. Belardo, *De Iuribus S.R.E. Cardinalium in Titulis*, Romae: Anonim. Libr. Cattolica Italiana, 1939.

CHAPTER II

INTRODUCTORY COMMENTARY TO CANON 239 § 1

Canon 239, § 1. Praeter alia privilegia quae in hoc Codice suis in titulis enumerantur, Cardinales omnes a sua promotione in Consistorio facultate gaudent. . . .

It is first stated in this canon that besides the many privileges that are subsequently enumerated in paragraph I, cardinals are the recipients of other privileges granted by the general law of the Code. These privileges are enumerated under the following canons: 223, § 1, n. 1, 600, § 3, 604, 728, § 3, 811, § 2, 812, 1155, § 1, 1189, 1401, 1414, § 4, 1432, § 1, 1557, § 1, 1770, § 2 and 2227, § 2. Accordingly, these privileges together with those enumerated in Canon 239, § 1 will be treated of in their proper place in this work.

Indicating the grantee of these privileges, the Canon uses the words "*Cardinales omnes,*" thereby clearly expressing that each and every cardinal whether he be a cardinal bishop, a cardinal priest or a cardinal deacon shares in and enjoys all of the privileges that are granted to cardinals by the Code. It should be noted here that the College of Cardinals is to be comprised of no more than seventy cardinals, the number having been set at seventy by Pope Sixtus V after the number of Elders in the Old Testament.[1] That number, however, is rarely realized at any time because of the changes caused by death. Of the seventy there are to be six cardinal bishops, fifty cardinal priests and fourteen cardinal deacons. The six cardinal bishops rule over the suburbicarian dioceses adjacent to Rome.[2] While there are only six cardinal bishops, there are seven suburbicarian Sees: Ostia, Velletri, Palestrina (Praeneste), Albano, Sabina, Frascati (Tusculum) and Porto-San Rufina (The Diocese of Santa Rufina was united to that of Porto in the twelfth century. It was also known as Silva Candida). Any difficulty in this regard is

[1] Const. "*Postquam,*" 3 dec. 1586, § 4—*Fontes,* n. 159.

[2] Canon 231, § 1.

obviated by the fact that each of the six cardinal bishops is appointed over one of these seven dioceses, while the Dean of the Cardinal College, who is always the oldest cardinal bishop in terms of promotion to one of the suburbicarian Sees,[3] always has Ostia besides the other diocese which he had when he became the dean of the College of Cardinals.[4] Once they have taken canonical possession of their dioceses, these cardinals are truly *Ordinarii locorum*, and have the same rights and duties as residential bishops.[5]

The fifty cardinal priests as well as the fourteen cardinal deacons are assigned to title churches and deaconries respectively in the City of Rome.[6] Although in their title churches and deaconries, cardinals lack jurisdiction over the faithful and cannot decide judicial matters, they have certain administrative and corrective powers and enjoy certain honorific rights.[7]

The present law makes the Priesthood a necessary qualification for the cardinalate.[8] That requirement, however, was not stipulated in pre-Code law. In earlier times when one was created a cardinal deacon, he was simply a deacon who was being elevated to the cardinalate. The same was true of a cardinal priest and of a cardinal bishop. Today, when a cardinal is created, it often happens that he is already a residential bishop in some part of the world. By his appointment he would not thereby become a cardinal bishop. His rank will be determined by the decree of his nomination. In such a case, it will generally be that of a cardinal priest, and while still remaining a residential bishop, he will be assigned a title church in Rome. For instance, His Eminence, Dennis Cardinal Dougherty,

[3] Canon 237, § 1.

[4] Canon 236, § 4.

[5] Canon 240, § 1.

[6] Canon 231, § 2. A *"Titulus"* is a church to which some cardinal is assigned. If taken in the wide sense it also comprehends Deaconries. In its proper sense, which is that of the Code, it refers only to a church to which a cardinal priest is assigned. There are in Rome 54 title churches and 16 deaconries. As is apparent, some are at times vacant. For the history of the term "title," the reader is referred to Christ, "The Origin and Development of the term *Title*,"—*The Jurist*, IV (1944), 101-123.

[7] Canon 240, § 2.

[8] Canon 232, § 1.

the present Ordinary of the Archdiocese of Philadelphia, while a residential archbishop, holds in the College of Cardinals the rank of a cardinal priest with the Title Church of Saints Nereus and Achilleus.

The canon further states that cardinals enjoy these privileges "*a sua promotione in Consistorio.*" This phrase signifies that from the moment his name is made public by the Pope to the other cardinals gathered in secret consistory, the new cardinal enjoys these privileges. For the creation of a cardinal all that is required is the will of the Sovereign Pontiff sufficiently expressed. It is usual that he express his will by announcing the names of the new cardinals to the cardinals who are present in Rome gathered in secret consistory.[9] The pontiff may, however, announce that he is creating a new cardinal but reserving his name *in pectore.*[10] In such a case the cardinal so created does not begin to enjoy the cardinalitial privileges until after the Pope has published his name. His precedence, however, will be reckoned from the time of the reservation *in pectore.*[11]

Therefore, in view of the wording of the canon, a newly created cardinal may begin to use the cardinalitial privileges immediately upon hearing of his nomination. He may use any and all of these privileges even before he has received the red biretta or gone to Rome, if he was absent when his name was made public, to participate in the various ceremonies that accompany the elevation of a priest to the cardinalate.[12]

Pope Eugene IV maintained that newly created cardinals were

[9] Canon 233. Cf. e. g., *AAS,* XXV (1933), 122.

[10] Cf. e. g., the case of Cardinal Tedeschini, one of the most recent examples of a reservation *in pectore.—AAS,* XXV (1933), 122; XXVII (1935), 459-461.

[11] Canon 233, § 2.

[12] The ceremonies connected with the conferral of the red biretta and red hat will be noted in the chapter on privileges of dress. The other ceremonies are the following: (1) the official *closing of the mouth,* signifying that the new cardinal is forbidden to speak in any formal gatherings of the cardinals until his mouth is *officially opened* in the same or another secret consistory; (2) *the conferral of the Cardinal's Ring;* (3) *assignment to a title church or deaconry* in Rome, and finally, (4) the *profession of faith* (canon 1406, §§ 1, 2). For a description of these ceremonies cf. *AAS,* XXV (1933), 139, 140; Baart, The Roman Court (Milwaukee, 1895), pp. 47-50.

not to be considered cardinals in the full sense of the word nor could they take part in papal elections until they had accepted all the insignia of the cardinalate, taken the oath, and gone through the ceremonies of closing and opening the mouth and been assigned to a title church.[13] Pius V, however, in a decree of January 26, 1571, declared that newly created cardinals are cardinals in the fullest sense of the term and obtain all cardinalitial rights the moment they are appointed in secret consistory.[14] In the Code the legislator has incorporated this decree of Pius V.[15] Therefore, the closing and opening of the mouth, the conferral of the insignia and the oath are ceremonies or solemnities which do not affect the perfection of the act of nomination.

Some practical consequences of this phrase *"a sua promotione in Consistorio,"* would be had if, for instance, a new American cardinal were created. If he chose to go to Rome by boat (upon reception of the red biretta he must take an oath to make the trip within a year unless legitimately detained),[16] he could board the boat wearing the pectoral cross, say Mass daily on a portable altar and allow any priest traveling with him to do the same, provided the priest had permission to say Mass at sea, hear any confessions making use of the extensive jurisdiction that is granted him, impart the many blessings for which faculties are granted, etc.

Paragraph I of Canon 239 then continues by enumerating most of the cardinalitial privileges.[17] These privileges may be classified into the following groups: [18]

A. The privilege contained under n. 1 is exclusively proper to the cardinalate.

B. The privileges contained under nn. 2-6 are absolutely proper to cardinals. The term *absolute* rather than exclusive is used be-

[13] Const. *"In eminenti,"* 26 oct. 1431, §§ 2, 3—*Bull. Rom.*, V, 2, 3.

[14] *Bull. Rom.*, VII, 881.

[15] Cf. canon 233, § 1.

[16] Canon 234. Cf. canon 2397 where it is stated that this binds *sub poena amissionis cardinalatus.*

[17] The writer does not here enumerate the long list of privileges as he will quote each section of the canon as he treats the individual privileges.

[18] Cf. Blat, *Commentarium Textus Codicis Iuris Canonici* (5 vols. in 7, Romae, 1921-1938), II (1921), n. 200 (henceforth cited as *Commentarium*).

cause bishops also enjoy these privileges but under certain limitations and conditions.

C. The privileges contained under nn. 7-12 are common to both bishops and cardinals.[19]

D. The privileges contained under nn. 13-16 are for cardinals *privilegia,* while for bishops they are *iura.*

E. The privileges contained under nn. 17-18 are sometimes enjoyed by others than bishops and cardinals, but by the cardinals in a more excellent manner.

F. The remaining privileges are exclusively proper to cardinals, but they are granted certain limitations and conditions.

[19] Cf. canon 349, § 1, n. 1.

CHAPTER III

PRIVILEGES OF DRESS AND ADDRESS

ARTICLE I. RED HAT, RED BIRETTA, RED ZUCCHETTO, RED GARMENT CLOAK, AND RING

CONFORMABLY to their exalted position in the Church, the cardinals have been conceded many privileges intended to give outward manifestation to their high dignity. One of these is their privilege of dress.

The first of these privileges of dress is the red hat. This hat is properly the sign of the cardinalitial dignity, and was granted to the cardinals by Pope Innocent IV in the year 1245, shortly after the First Council of Lyons.[1] There is no foundation for the contention that it was granted the cardinals *at* the Council itself.[2] The red hat is solemnly conferred upon a newly created cardinal by the Pope himself at a public consistory following the new cardinal's promotion.[3] At the death of a cardinal this hat must be placed at the foot of the catafalque and, afterwards, suspended from the ceiling above his tomb.[4]

The *red biretta,* the *red skull-cap* (called also *calotte* or *zucchetto*), the *red cloak or mantle* were bestowed upon the cardinals by Pope Paul II (1464-1471).[5]

[1] Cf. Sägmüller, *Lehrbuch des katholischen Kirchenrechts,* vol. I, 526; Hinschius, *System des katholischen Kirchenrechts,* I, 358, n. 4; Hilling, *Procedure at the Roman Curia,* 29; P. M. Baumgarten, "Die Ubersendung des Roten Hutes,"—*Historisches Jahrbuch* (Im Auftrage der Görres-Gesellschaft, Munster, 1880-1882; München, 1883-1919), XXV (1905), 99 ff.

[2] Cf. Kuttner, "Die Konstitutionen des ersten allgemeinen Konzils von Lyon,"—*Studia et Documenta Historiae et Iuris* (Romae; Apollinaris, 1935—), VI (1940), 120-124.

[3] Cf. e.g., *AAS,* XXVIII (1936), 224.

[4] Cf. Nainfa, *Costume of Prelates of the Catholic Church* (Baltimore: John Murphy Co., 1926), p. 106.

[5] Cf. Sägmüller, *loc. cit.;* Hilling, *loc. cit.* Some earlier authors main-

If a newly appointed cardinal is present in Rome, the *red biretta* is imposed by the Pope himself several days after the new cardinal's name has been made public.[6] If the cardinal is not in Rome, then the biretta is carried to him by a legate appointed for this specific purpose. Should the newly appointed cardinal pertain to a Catholic country, then the duly appointed ruler of that State imposes the red biretta on the cardinal.[7] Otherwise it is imposed on the cardinal by the legate who brings it. The biretta ordinarily worn by a cardinal is not the one he receives from the Pope. Out of respect for its origin cardinals do not wear that biretta, but should place it on a credence table in their ante-chamber, between two candlesticks.[8]

It may also be noted here that until the pontificate of Leo XIII, the biretta of cardinals was red, while that of all the other members of the clergy, including bishops, was uniformly black. However, since a large number of bishops and other prelates had presumed to wear the purple biretta, Leo XIII enacted new legislation, granting to all patriarchs, primates, archbishops and bishops the exclusive privilege of wearing a purple biretta.[9]

The *red skull-cap* (*calotte* or *zucchetto*) is another of the proper insignia of the cardinalate together with the red hat and red biretta. It is so exclusively reserved to cardinals, that the Pope, when grant-

tained that these privileges of dress were granted by Boniface VIII (1294-1303), but Plati and Hilling both claim that Paul II was the grantor. Sägmüller states that the wearing of the *red garment* began under Boniface VIII, but that the cloak or mantle was given them by Paul II.

[6] Cf. e. g., *AAS,* XXV (1933), 122, 123.

[7] An example of this was had in the case of Cardinal Piffl, Prince-Archbishop of Vienna, who was created a cardinal on May 25, 1914. The red biretta was imposed on him by Archduke Franz Ferdinand in Vienna on June 6, 1914—cf. *Archiv für katholisches Kirchenrechts* (Innsbruck, 1857-1861; Mainz, 1862—), XCIV (1914), 518 (henceforth cited as *AKKR*). The most recent example of this is the case of Cardinal Tedeschini, who at the time of his elevation to the cardinalate (his name was made public Dec. 16, 1935, having been reserved *in pectore* on March 13, 1933) was Papal Nuncio to Spain. The red biretta was imposed on him in 1936 by the President of the Republic in Madrid.

[8] Cf. Nainfa, *op. cit.*, p. 111.

[9] Const. *"Praeclaro divinae gratiae,"* 3 feb. 1888—*Acta Sanctae Sedis* (Romae, 1865-1908), XX (1887-1888), 369. (Henceforth cited as *ASS.*)

ing, by special favor, to a bishop the privilege of wearing a cardinal's robes without making him a cardinal, always excepts the use of the red skull-cap.[10] The Code allows cardinals to wear the skull-cap while celebrating Mass.[11] From the *Sanctus* until after the Communion, however, the skull-cap is to be removed out of reverence for the sacred mysteries then being performed. It should never be worn in the presence of the Blessed Sacrament exposed. Cardinals, however, of all ecclesiastical prelates have the exclusive privilege of wearing the skull-cap in the presence of the Sovereign Pontiff. All other prelates remain bareheaded in his presence, and even cardinals when bowing to him must momentarily remove the skull-cap.[12]

Since the reign of Gregory XIV (1591), the three insignia of the red hat, red biretta and red skull-cap may also be worn by cardinals belonging to religious orders. In their other apparel they retain the color used for the habit of the order to which they belong. However, the custom of using the same *form* as that of a secular cardinal's costume is tolerated.[13] Thus, clerics of Religious Orders properly so called, such as Benedictines, Carmelites, Dominicans, Franciscans, etc., when raised to the cardinalate, will adopt for their costume the color proper to their Order, while Clerics Regular, as Jesuits, Redemptorists, Theatines, etc., adopt for their costume that of secular cardinals.[14]

Another of the distinctive insignia of the cardinalate is the *Cardinal's Ring*. This they receive from the Pope at a secret consistory soon after their promotion.[15] This ring is adorned with a

[10] Cf. Nainfa, *op. cit.*, pp. 114, 115. The Prince-Archbishop of Salzburg is one example of a bishop having the privilege of wearing the cardinals' garb. A similar privilege was conceded to the Prince-Primates of Hungary, Poland and Germany, to wear the cardinals' garb even if they had not been promoted to the cardinalate. Cf. L. Sajó, "Der Purpur des Fürst—Primas von Ungarn,"—*AKKR*, LXXVII (1892), 433.

[11] Canon 811, § 2.

[12] Nainfa, *op. cit.*, pp. 117, 118.

[13] Cf. Nainfa, *op. cit.*, pp. 17-20. The decree of Gregory XIV was published in a secret consistory of April 26, 1591—quoted by Plati, *De Cardinalis Dignitate et Officio*, p. 50.

[14] Cf. Nainfa, *loc. cit.*

[15] Cf. e. g., *AAS*, XXV (1933), 139, 140.

sapphire (a stone reserved for cardinals) and has engraved inside the coat-of-arms of the pontiff who created the ecclesiastic a cardinal. Cardinals may wear the ring (ordinarily it is not this one, but either the pontifical or the ordinary ring)[16] when celebrating Mass.[17] It is worthy of note that on March 18, 1909, Pius X granted an indulgence of fifty days to anyone kissing the ring of a cardinal or a bishop.[18] In kissing the ring of any cardinal outside of Rome, one should first genuflect out of respect for the cardinal's dignity. In the city of Rome, however, out of respect for the person of the Pope, this procedure should not be followed.[19]

The other garments worn by cardinals include the *simar* (house-cassock), the *red choir cassock,* the *red cincture,* the *rochet,* the *mantelletta,* the *mozzetta* and the *cappa magna.*[20]

Article II. Pectoral Cross, Mitre and Crozier

Canon 239, § 1, n. 13. More Episcoporum gestandi crucem ante pectus etiam supra mozetam atque utendi mitra et baculo pastorali.

The *pectoral cross* has always been one of the distinctive insignia of bishops. By this section of canon 239, § 1, however, all cardinals, even those who are not endowed with the episcopal character are privileged to wear the pectoral cross.

This privilege was granted the cardinals by Pius X on May 24, 1905. In his decree the pontiff stated that although the pectoral cross was a distinctive sign of a bishop, indults had been granted at various times both to secular and regular dignitaries to make use of it under certain specific limitations. In view of these facts, and because of the high dignity of the cardinalate, he conceded to

[16] Cf. Nainfa, *Costume of Prelates,* pp. 38, 39.

[17] Canon 811, § 2.

[18] *AAS,* I (1909), 277.

[19] Cf. *The Clergy Review* (London, 1931—), XII (1936), 338.

[20] For a description and history of these garments and the appropriate times at which they are to be worn, the reader is referred to Nainfa, *Costume of Prelates,* pp. 210-213.

all cardinals the privilege of wearing it at all times and with no limitations.[21]

This section of Canon 239, § 1 further grants to cardinals the privilege of using the *mitre* and *crozier*. This privilege was enjoyed by cardinals prior to the Code, but for use in their title churches or deaconries only. The unrestricted use of the mitre and crozier without the permission of the local ordinary, is a privilege that is new with the Code.

The *mitre* is usually a sign of episcopal dignity. Since the cardinalitial dignity is higher than that of the episcopate, the cardinals' privilege in this regard is readily understandable. Since bishops may wear the mitre even outside their territorial jurisdiction,[22] the cardinals' unrestricted use of it follows *a fortiori*.

The *crozier*, however, is a token of jurisdiction. Bishops, therefore, may not use it outside their own territory without the express, or at the very least, the reasonably presumed permission of the local ordinary.[23]

Since cardinals assist the pontiff in the government of the universal Church,[24] they may make use of the crozier in all places without the necessity of the local Ordinary's permission. Moreover, they may make use of the crozier even in the churches of the city of Rome, the patriarchal basilicas alone being excepted. This was declared in a response of the Pontifical Commission for the Interpretation of the Code under date of May 29, 1934.[25]

This response, according to Maroto, was based on the fact that the patriarchal basilicas are under the immediate, proper and exclusive power and jurisdiction of the Roman Pontiff. These basilicas are to the Roman Pontiff what the cathedral church is to a residential bishop. The Lateran Basilica is his cathedral church, while the others can be likened to his co-cathedrals.[26]

[21] Motu propr. "*Crux pectoralis*," 24 maii 1905—*Fontes*, n. 669.

[22] Cf. *Caeremoniale Episcoporum*, Liber I, cap. XVII.

[23] Cf. canon 337, § 1; *Caeremoniale Episcoporum*, I, cap. XVII.

[24] Canon 230.

[25] *AAS*, XXVI (1934), 493; Reported in Bouscaren, *The Canon Law Digest* [2 vols., Milwaukee: Bruce Publishing Co., Vol. I (1934), Vol. II (1943)], II, 95. (Hereafter cited as Bouscaren, *Digest*.)

[26] Cf. Maroto, in *Apollinaris*, VIII (1935), 46-54. The patriarchal basilicas

Maroto, in further explaining the restriction of this privilege by the above-mentioned response of the Code Commission, gives an interpretation that, if carried to its logical conclusion, would too greatly restrict the cardinals' privilege of using the crozier. He asserts that since the canon in question uses the words *"more episcoporum,"* this privilege of cardinals is subject to the same limitations of the *Caeremoniale Episcoporum* as is the similar privilege of bishops.[27]

In view of section 15 of this same canon, together with canon 240, § 3,[28] such an interpretation seems too restricted to the writer. As has been noted, the crozier is a sign of jurisdiction. For a residential bishop to use it outside of his proper diocese, he needs, according to canon 337, § 1, the consent, at least reasonably presumed, of the local Ordinary, together with, if the church is an exempt one, the consent of the religious superior.[29] Although Canon 337, § 1 does not use the word *baculum,* from the definition of the phrase *"exercere pontificalia"* given in paragraph II of the same canon,[30] it is readily seen that *baculum* is implicitly contained in the phrase *"exercere pontificalia"* of paragraph I. Therefore, to use the crozier outside their proper diocese, bishops need the local Ordinary's consent.

That cardinals are not bound to this restriction is evident from section 15 of canon 239, § 1, and from canon 240, § 3. Although these two canons are directly concerned with the use of the throne and baldachine at pontifical functions, they also indicate that cardinals may use the crozier (*"pontificalia peragendi"*) in all churches

of Rome are the four Major Basilicas: St. John Lateran's, St. Peter's, St. Paul's outside the walls, and St. Mary Major's.

27 "Commentarium in Responsum P.C.I. ad Can. 239, § 1, nn. 12, 13, 24."—*Apollinaris,* VIII (1935), 50-51.

28 Cf. below, p. 28.

29 Episcopus in tota dioecesi, ne exceptis quidem locis exemptis, potest pontificalia exercere; non vero extra dioecesim sine expresso vel saltem rationabiliter praesumpto consensu Ordinarii loci, et, si agatur de ecclesia exempta, de consensu Superioris religiosi.

30 *Exercere pontificalia* in iure est sacras functiones peragere quae ex legibus liturgicis requirunt insignia pontificalia, idest *baculum* et mitram.

outside of Rome without the need of any local Ordinary's consent.[81] *In the City of Rome,* they may use the crozier (*"pontificalia peragere"*) in all churches except the four patriarchal basilicas.[82]

In view of these canons it may be concluded that the cardinals' privilege of using the crozier is not, as Maroto would have it, subject to the limitations of the *Caeremoniale Episcoporum.*[83]

ARTICLE III. PRIVILEGE OF USING THE THRONE AND BALDACHINE [84]

Canon 239, § 1, n. 15. Pontificalia cum throno et baldachino peragendi in omnibus ecclesiis extra urbem, Ordinario praemonito, si ecclesia sit cathedralis.

Canon 240, § 3. Cum throno et baldachino Cardinalis ordinis presbyteralis potest in suo titulo pontificalia peragere et Cardinalis ordinis diaconalis in sua diaconia pontificaliter assistere, et nemo alius ibidem id potest sine Cardinalis assensu; in aliis vero Urbis ecclesiis Cardinalis throno et baldachino uti nequent sine licentia Romani Pontificis.

Intimately connected with the privilege of using the mitre and crozier is the privilege of performing pontifical functions *using the throne* and *canopy or baldachine.* It has been noted in the foregoing article that *"peragere pontificalia"* implies the use of the

[81] Canon 239, § 1, n. 15. To use the throne and baldachine at the same time, cardinals must, if the church is a cathedral church, make known their intention to the local Ordinary, but do not need his consent.

[82] Cf. canon 240, § 2, together with the above-mentioned response of the Code Commission which excepts the patriarchal basilicas. Outside their title churches or deaconries, cardinals may not use the throne and baldachine in Rome without the permission of the Sovereign Pontiff.

[83] The words *"more Episcoporum"* upon which Maroto bases his interpretation, seem to refer rather to the pectoral cross, which up until the time of Pius X's decree (*"Crux pectoralis,"* 24 maii, 1905) had been proper to bishops alone.

[84] Although not a privilege of dress, this privilege is being treated here because of its intimate association with the use of the pontifical insignia of mitre and crozier.

crozier, which is a sign of jurisdiction.[85] The pontifical functions are performed in the celebration of Solemn Mass, at pontifical Vespers, in pontifically assisting at Mass or the choral recitation of the Office, in the conferring of Orders, in the consecration of a bishop, the blessing of an abbot, the consecration of churches, bells and sacred utensils, the blessing of a corner-stone or a cemetery, in the reconciliation of a church or cemetery and in the conferring of Confirmation.[86]

According to these two canons, exclusive of the use of the throne and baldachine, cardinals may perform the pontifical functions in all churches of the world, excluding only the four patriarchal basilicas. They may use the *throne and canopy* outside of Rome in any church, but should it be a cathedral church they should make known their intention to the Ordinary. They do not, however, need his consent. Within the City of Rome, they may use the throne and canopy in their title churches or deaconries; to use it in other churches of Rome, they must first get the papal permission.[87]

This privilege is another that was formerly enjoyed by cardinals for use only in their titles or deaconries.[88] The use of it outside these churches was referred to in a response given prior to the Code by the Sacred Congregation of Rites, but no express concession of it in written form is contained in the pre-Code legislation. Custom, then, would seem to have been the determining factor for its use prior to the Code. That the cardinals enjoyed such a privilege was presupposed in a response of the Congregation of Rites under date of July 14, 1887. The Congregation was asked whether a cardinal celebrating Mass *in pontificals outside of Rome* and *outside of a*

[85] *Exercere seu peragere pontificalia* is one thing; *uti pontificalibus* is another. The latter implies the use of the buskins, sandals, tunics, gemmed ring, gloves, pectoral cross, gremial and simple mitre; *but not the crozier.* Cf. Beste, *Introductio in Codicem* (Collegeville, Minn.: St. John's Abbey Press, 1938), p. 268.

[86] Cf. S.C.C., 9-11 feb. 1924,—*AAS,* XVII (1925), 245.

[87] Cf. also the instruction of the Sacred Ceremonial Congregation dated Dec. 2, 1930, which lays down special rules to be followed by the cardinals in accepting invitations to perform pontifical functions in Rome, but outside of their titles or deaconries—*AAS,* XXIII (1931), 57-59.

[88] Cf. above, p. 14.

place under his jurisdiction, could have, besides the three ministers of the altar, vested deacons *assisting at the throne.* The Congregation replied in the affirmative.[39] This response indicated that the use of the throne by a cardinal outside of a place under his jurisdiction was an accepted privilege of the cardinalate.

The general rule to which the cardinals' privilege is a favorable exception is that residential bishops, from the time they have taken canonical possession of their diocese have the right of erecting in all churches of their diocese, including those of exempt religious, a throne with canopy or baldachine.[40] Outside their dioceses, however, they need the consent of the local Ordinary.[41]

Article IV. Privilege of Address

Another privilege designed to manifest externally the exalted dignity of the cardinalate is their privilege of being addressed as "*Eminence.*"

Historically, the use of this title of address dates back to the early seventeenth century, when the Sacred Congregation of Ceremonies under Urban VIII (1623-1644) issued on June 10, 1630, a decree stating that the titles *eminentia, eminentissime* and *vestra eminentia,* along with *reverendissime* which was already in use, were from that day forward to be the proper and exclusive titles of the cardinalitial dignity.[42]

This privilege cardinals enjoy to this day. It may be here noted in passing that while Germany was under the head of the Nazi Party, the Reich Minister for Ecclesiastical Affairs forbade the use of this

[39] S.R.C., *Neapolitana,* 14 iul. 1887, I—*Fontes,* n. 6184.

[40] Canon 349, § 2, n. 3.

[41] Cf. canon 337, § 3; *Caeremoniale Episcoporum,* I, cap. XIII; S.R.C., 26 nov. 1919, ad III, nn. 4, 5, 6—*AAS,* XII (1920), 182.

[42] Cf. "Dignité des Cardinauz"—*Analecta Iuris Pontificii,* II (1857), 1921-1922. The decree of the Sacred Congregation is quoted in this article. The Grand Master of the Knights of Malta, although a layman, is also privileged to be addressed as *eminentia.* This exception was noted in the decree of June 10, 1630. The three Archbishop Electors of the Holy Roman Empire were also formerly privileged to use the same title.

title in addressing a cardinal. The decree states that in all official letters addressed to cardinals, archbishops or bishops, only the following titles are to be used in the future: "*Kardinal*," "*Erzbischof*" or "*Bischof*." All other titles such as "*Eminenz*" or "*Exzellenz*" were to be omitted.[43]

[43] This decree is reported in the *Frankfurter Zeitung*, n. 604 (1938). Cf. *AKKR*, CXIX (1939), 249.

CHAPTER IV

PRIVILEGE OF PRECEDENCE

Canon 239, § 1, n. 21. Praecedendi omnibus Praelatis etiam Patriarchis, imo ipsis Legatis Pontificiis, nisi Legatus sit Cardinalis in proprio territorio residens; Cardinalis autem Legatus a latere praecedit extra Urbem omnibus aliis.

THE present law states that cardinals, even though not bishops, are privileged to precede all prelates, even patriarchs and papal legates, unless the papal legate is also a cardinal, in which case he precedes all cardinals within the territory of his jurisdiction. Outside the City of Rome, a cardinal legate *a latere* takes precedence over all other cardinals.

Precedence may be defined canonically as the external attestation of greater honor and reverence which is due one group or individual rather than another in public prayers, processions, meetings, etc., with regard to the order of entering, seating, voting or signing.[1]

The excellence upon which the right of precedence is founded is either personal or derivative accordingly as the reason for it is founded on some personal dignity or is otherwise derived from the person one represents. This in the course of time has given rise to many controversies. The occasion of many of these disputes was the fact that there is in the Church a double hierarchy, namely, a hierarchy of orders and a hierarchy of jurisdiction.[2] Priority in one does not necessarily carry with it the same prerogative in the other. As will be seen this was the underlying factor in the early disputes over precedence between bishops, who were more excellent by reason of the hierarchy of orders, and cardinals, who were more excellent by reason of dignity. Good order demands that everyone be shown the honor that is his due and that futile and scandalous controversies

[1] Cf. Beste, *Introductio in Codicem*, p. 162.
[2] Canon 108, § 3.

be avoided. It is necessary, therefore, to have canonical criteria by which to judge all questions of precedence.

The general norms of ecclesiastical precedence are stipulated in canon 106. Special legislation, however, is had for cardinals and it is contained in section 21 of canon 239.

This privilege is by no means new. It has a long history filled with many disputes as to whether a cardinal precedes a bishop, or a bishop a cardinal.[3]

Up to the eleventh century, a bishop took precedence over a cardinal.[4] Previous to that, the question of precedence had been determined by the concept of orders rather than by that of dignity. By reasons of orders a bishop ranked higher than a cardinal, for in the ecclesiastical hierarchy of Orders there is no order higher than the episcopate. Gradually, however, the concept of orders began to give place to that of dignity in the question of precedence. The facts that brought about this change were the following:

1. The fact that Nicholas II in 1059 constituted cardinals as the principal electors in the election of the Roman Pontiff.[5]

2. The fact that cardinals were most frequently sent as legates to Councils and Princes. When so sent, even though they were merely priests or deacons, they preceded bishops e. g. in signing the decrees of the Council. Because of this the observance of the precedence of bishops began to cede place to the recognition of the dignity of the cardinalate. Cardinal-bishops began to precede bishops who were not cardinals, and soon this precedence passed also the cardinal-priests and cardinal-deacons, who with the cardinal-bishops constituted one body.[6]

3. The fact that Innocent IV, shortly after the First General

[3] The history of this privilege is taken up at length by Vincentius Card. Petra, *Commentaria ad Constitutiones Apostolicas* (5 tom. in 2 vols., Venetiis, 1729), I, 78 sq. (*Commentarium in Constitutionem Unicam Joannis XV*).

[4] This is evident e.g. from the subscriptions to the Constitution *"Cum Conventus"* of John XV (985-996)—cf. Card. Petra, *op. cit.*, I, 78.

[5] C. 1. D. XXIII: " . . . statuimus, ut obeunte huius Romanae venerabilis ecclesiae pontifice, imprimis Cardinales episcopi diligentissime simul de electione tractantes, mox Christi clericos Cardinales adhibeant: sicque reliquus clericus et populus ad consensum novae electionis accedat; . . . "

[6] Cf. Card. Petra, *op. cit.*, I, 89.

Council of Lyons (1245), granted cardinals the insignia of honor and dignity, the red hat.[7]

In the II General Council of Lyons (1274) cardinals preceded patriarchs, primates, metropolitans, bishops and all other prelates.[8] Disputes, however, still arose and an outstanding one led to the decree *Non mediocri* of Eugene IV, establishing definitely the precedence of cardinals over bishops and all other prelates.[9] Later pontiffs corroborated this decree of Eugene IV [10] and it is on this decree that the present law of the Code is based.

This question of precedence is best viewed from the standpoint of a twofold distinction: (1) the precedence of cardinals over all other clerics; (2) the precedence of cardinals over one another.

Article I. The Precedence of Cardinals Over All Other Clerics [11]

Cardinals hold above all other ecclesiastics a more eminent position immediately under the Roman Pontiff. They are entitled to this position for they constitute the Senate of the Church and are the Pope's principal counsellors and advisors.[12] By reason of this privilege any cardinal will take precedence in any part of the world over all other non-cardinals, whether these latter be patriarchs, primates, archbishops, bishops or even papal legates.[13]

[7] Cf. above, p. 22.

[8] Cf. Hardouin, VII, 670.

[9] Promulgated in the year 1439—*Fontes,* n. 50.

[10] Leo X, Const. *"Supernae,"* 5 maii, 1514—*Fontes,* n. 15: " . . . sanctae romanae Ecclesiae Cardinales coeteros omnes in ipsa Ecclesia, post Summum Pontificem, honore ac dignitate praecedant . . . "; Sixtus V, *"Postquam,"* 3 dec. 1586—*Fontes,* n. 159; Conc. Trident., sess. XXIV, *de ref.,* cap. 11—Schroeder, *op. cit.,* p. 199; Pius IX, *"Multiplices,"* 27 nov. 1869—*Fontes,* n. 553.

[11] With regard to laymen, the cardinals' precedence is determined from the fact that they are considered princes. They, therefore, cede place only to kings and are equal rank with princes of royal families. (Wernz, *Ius Decretalium,* II, 634, II.) Their princely prerogative is expressly recognized in the concordat between Italy and the Holy See, wherein (Art. XXI) it is stated that in Italy all cardinals enjoy the honors and prerogatives that are enjoyed by the Princes of the reigning royal family. Cf. *AAS,* XXI (1929), 219.

[12] Canon 230.

[13] Canons 239, § 1, n. 21; 280; 347 and 269, § 2.

This right to precedence is fittingly called a privilege, for it is a favorable exception to the general norms of precedence enumerated in canon 106. The general law states that he who represents another person takes precedence according to the rank of the person he represents.[14] Accordingly, a papal legate who is not a cardinal, should, since he represents the Roman Pontiff, take precedence over any cardinal. Such is not the case, since cardinals *are privileged* by canon 239 to precede all other ecclesiastics including papal legates who are not cardinals.

Article II. The Precedence of Cardinals Among Themselves

A. General Norms

The precedence of one cardinal over another is a question of no little import. According to the Code any doubts in this regard are to be settled according to the following norms.

The Dean of the Sacred College who is the oldest cardinal in years of promotion to a suburbicarian see, precedes all other cardinals.[15] Next to the Dean in order of precedence comes the Sub-Dean of the Sacred College.[16] For the other cardinals, the principal criterion is that of the Order to which they pertain. Those that belong to a higher order precede those who pertain to an inferior order.[17] Cardinal bishops, therefore, precede cardinal priests, while the latter take precedence over cardinal deacons.[18]

Within the same order precedence ordinarily follows according to the number of years that a cardinal has belonged to a given order of the cardinalate.[19] Thus, for instance, of two cardinal priests, the one who has been a cardinal-priest, not simply a cardinal, for

[14] Canon 106, n. 1.

[15] Canon 237, § 1.

[16] Canon 237, § 2.

[17] Canon 106, n. 3.

[18] It may be here mentioned that in a pontifical procession the various orders of the Sacred College wear distinguishing garments. The Cardinal bishops vest in the cope; the cardinal priests in the chasuble, and the cardinal deacons in the dalmatic. Cf. Nainfa, *Costume of Prelates*, pp. 93-94.

[19] Canon 106, n. 3.

the greater number of years will generally take precedence over the other. There is one exception to this rule: It is had when a cardinal, after ten years as a cardinal-deacon, transfers *by option* in accordance with the norms laid down, to the order of cardinal-priest.[20] Following the transfer, such a cardinal will take precedence over all cardinal priests who were created cardinals after the cardinal in question was raised to the cardinalate.[21] Although the other cardinal-priests in question have been cardinal-priests longer than the cardinal who transferred to the order by option, nevertheless, he is privileged to precede them on the basis of his seniority in the cardinalitial college.[22]

If the norms of order and seniority fail as in the case of two ecclesiastics having been promoted to the same order of the cardinalate on the same day, then precedence is to be decided first according to superiority in Sacred Orders. Thus, if a bishop and a priest were on the same day, promoted to the cardinalate with the rank of cardinal-priests, the bishop would take precedence over the simple priest.

If there is equality in Sacred Orders, then seniority of ordination becomes the criterion. Thus, if two bishops are created cardinals on the same day, the one who had been consecrated earlier would take precedence. If the case concerned two priests, the one who had been ordained earlier would precede the other. If this criterion also fails, then the one who is older in years of age takes precedence. This would be required in the case of two priests who had been ordained on the same day being promoted to the same order of the cardinalate at the same consistory.[23]

There is another important exception to the norms of order and seniority governing this precedence. That is had in the case of the cardinal who is also a residential bishop. He, within the territory of

[20] Canon 236, § 1.

[21] Canon 236, § 2, together with response of PCI under date of May 29, 1934—*AAS,* XXVI (1934), 493; Bouscaren, *Digest,* II, 95.

[22] The Code in this matter has incorporated as Canon 236, § 2, a decree of Pope Clement VIII (1592-1605)—*Bull. Rom.,* X, 364.

[23] Canon 106, n. 3. Cf. Maroto, *Institutiones Iuris Canonici,* Vol. II, Tom. II (Matriti, 1919), n. 816.

his jurisdiction, precedes all other cardinals, no matter what their order or seniority, except a cardinal legate *a latere*.[24]

B. The Precedence of Cardinal Legates

With regard to cardinal legates and their precedence, it may be noted here that the pontiffs have made use of legates to carry out important missions for many centuries. In the period of the decretals three types of legates are mentioned: *legati missi, legati nati* and *legati a latere*.[25] Cardinals, says Schmalzgrueber, were selected for carrying out the more important and arduous missions.[26] Moreover, cardinals were exclusively selected as legates *a latere*.[27]

The powers of *legati a latere* were based analogically on those of the Roman Law *Proconsules,* while those of the *legati missi* and the *legati nati* were similar to those of the *Praesides provinciarum* of Roman Law.[28] Legates *a latere* had much more jurisdiction than the other two classes of legates, especially in absolving from reserved censures and the conferring of benefices.[29]

Since cardinals were exclusively selected as legates *a latere,* and since legates *a latere* enjoyed greater powers of jurisdiction, it can be readily seen that they took precedence over all other legates. And, since cardinals as such had precedence over bishops and other prelates, it was but logical that the added distinction of being appointed legate *a latere* would give such a cardinal precedence outside of Rome over everyone, for, as Eugene IV stated, such cardinals

[24] Cf. Toso, *Ad Codicem Iuris Canonici Commentaria Minora* (5 vols., 1920-1934), Vol. II, Tom. II (Romae, 1923), p. 43; hereafter cited *Commentaria*.

[25] Cf. X, *de officio legati* I, 30; *de officio legati* I, 15, in VI°.

[26] *Ius Ecclesiasticum Universum* (5 vols. in 12, Romae, 1843-1845), Lib. I, tit. XXX, *de officio legati*, n. 1.

[27] Cf. X, *de officio legati* I, 30, especially c. 9 with gloss s. v. *commissam*; X, *de officio legati* I, 15, in VI°, especially c. 1 with introductory gloss, in which Ioannes Andreae stated that this class was so reserved because with the pope the cardinals formed "unum corpus," of which the pope is the "caput" and they are "membra."

[28] C. 2, *de officio legati* I, 15, in VI°.

[29] C. 20, X, *de sententia excommunicationis* V, 39. Today, their powers depend on their pontifical commission (canon 266).

are then acting directly for the Pope and honor shown them is actually being shown to the Pope.[80]

The present legislation on cardinal legates and their precedence decrees that if a cardinal is sent as a papal legate not, however, *a latere,* he then precedes all other prelates including other cardinals, but only *when he is within the territory of his jurisdiction.* Outside that territory his precedence among other cardinals will be determined according to the general norms of order and seniority within a given order.[81]

A legate *a latere* is always a cardinal sent on a special mission as the *alter ego* of the Roman Pontiff.[82] He is privileged by law to precede outside of Rome all other prelates including cardinals who might be his senior by reason of order or years within a given order.[83] Hence, when present with other cardinals the ordinary norms of precedence, namely, the order to which he pertains or seniority within that order, are waived. The canon uses the words *"extra Urbem."* Therefore, within the City of Rome no recognition is given to the added quality of legate. The reason for this is that the designated cardinal does not begin to enjoy his rights and privileges as legate until the moment he passes through the city gates and is actually on his mission.

Finally, in the question of cardinalitial precedence it is to be noted that if the Pope in a secret consistory declares that he is creating a new cardinal but reserving his name *in pectore* until a later date, the cardinal so created begins to enjoy the cardinalitial privileges only from the day on which his name is made public. His precedence in the Sacred College, however, will date from the day of the papal *reservatio in pectore.*[84]

[80] Const. *"Non mediocri,"* § 7—*Fontes,* n. 50.

[81] Cf. canon 239, § 1, n. 21.

[82] Canon 266.

[83] Canon 239, § 1, n. 21.

[84] Canon 233, § 2.

CHAPTER V

PRIVILEGES THAT CONCERN THE ADMINISTRATION AND RECEPTION OF CERTAIN SACRAMENTS

Article I. The Extensive Jurisdiction of Cardinals As Confessors

Canon 239, § 1, n. 1. Audiendi ubique terrarum confessiones etiam religiosorum utriusque sexus et absolvendi ab omnibus peccatis et censuris etiam reservatis, exceptis tantum censuris Sedi Apostolicae specialissimo modo reservatis et illis quae adnexae sunt revelationi secreti S. Officii.

Canon 873, § 1. Ordinaria iurisdictione ad confessiones excipiendas pro universa Ecclesia, praeter Romanum Pontificem, potiuntur S.R.E. Cardinales: pro suo quisque territorio Ordinarius loci, et parochus aliique qui loco parochi sunt.

The privilege to be dealt with here, considered from the viewpoint of the members of the Church, both lay and clerical, is the most extensive of all the cardinalitial privileges since it concerns the many faculties that a cardinal enjoys to absolve from sins and censures in the act of sacramental confession.

Section 1. Introductory Commentary on the Ordinary Confessional Jurisdiction of Cardinals

Members of the College of Cardinals possess *ordinary* jurisdiction for the internal sacramental forum, over all the faithful, and are privileged to grant valid absolution from most sins and censures even though reserved, anywhere in the world and to any member of the Church.[1]

[1] Cf. canons 873, § 1; 239, § 1. This privilege is one of most recent origin. It was one of the privileges conceded to cardinals in anticipation of the Code

Canon 873, § 1 states that cardinals enjoy *ordinary* jurisdiction, which is defined in the Code as that jurisdiction which is annexed to an office by the law itself (*ipso iure*).[2]

In view of the fact that ordinary jurisdiction is annexed to the cardinalate, it is to be considered an office in the strict sense, since it fulfills all the requirements for such.[3] The fact that this ordinary jurisdiction annexed to the cardinalate is annexed by way of privilege, in no way argues against this conclusion, since the privilege by which it is annexed is one contained in the common law. The jurisdiction or power is therefore annexed to the cardinalate by the law itself (*ipso iure*). This would not be true of a privilege that is not contained within the common law, since such a privilege in no way partakes of the nature of a law.[4] Nor does the fact that this ordinary jurisdiction is an extrinsic addition to the cardinalate that is by no means essential, militate against the validity of the conclusion that the cardinalate is an office in the strict sense. Canon 197 [5] makes no distinction as to whether the power be essential or non-essential to the office, and, according to the accepted axiom, *"ubi lex non distinguit, nec nos distinguere debemus."* [6]

by Pope Pius X on December 11, 1920. (Cf. above, p. 10). Prior to that, members of the College of Cardinals never enjoyed such extensive faculties. Cf. *Razon y Fe*, XXXIII (1912), 243, n. 1. Bishops do not enjoy this privilege.

[2] Canon 197, § 1: Potestas iurisdictionis ordinaria ea est quae ipso iure adnexa est officio; delegata, quae commissa est personae.

[3] Canon 145: Officium ecclesiasticum lato sensu est quod libet munus quod in spiritualem finem legitime exercetur; stricto autem sensu est munus ordinatione sive divina sive ecclesiastica stabiliter constitutum, ad normam sacrorum canonum conferendum, aliquam saltem secumferens participationem ecclesiasticae potestatis sive ordinis sive iurisdictionis.

[4] Cf. Kearney, *Principles of Delegation*, the Catholic University of America Canon Law Studies, n. 55 (Washington, D. C.: The Catholic University of America, 1929), p. 54; Blat, *Commentarium*, III, Pars I (2. ed., Romae: Apud Angelicum, 1924), n. 196; Coronata, *Institutiones Iuris Canonici* (5 vols., Taurini: Marietti, 1928-1936), I (1928), n. 278 (henceforth cited as *Institutiones*).

[5] Quoted above in footnote n. 2.

[6] Cf. Kearney, *op. cit.*, pp. 63-64; Vermeersch-Creusen, *Epitome Iuris Canonici* (3 vols., Mechliniae, Romae: H. Dessain, 1934-1937), I (6. ed., 1937), 260, 261 (henceforth cited as *Epitome*).

This ordinary confessional jurisdiction that is annexed to the cardinalitial office cannot, however, be delegated to another by a cardinal.[7] Since such jurisdiction is ordinary it would seem that, in accordance with the norms of canon 199, § 1, such jurisdiction could be delegated.[8] Canon 199, § 1 contains the phrase *"nisi aliud expresse iure caveatur."* Accordingly, the delegation of ordinary jurisdiction is prohibited by law, only when the law makes express mention of such a prohibition. Neither in canon 873, § 1, nor in canon 239, § 1, n. 1 is express mention made of any such prohibition. However, such a prohibition of delegation may be *expressed* either *explicitly or implicitly.*[9] Although no explicit prohibition against a cardinal's delegating his ordinary confessional jurisdiction is found in the Code, the Code does contain an implicit one. In canons 874 and 875, the legislator has determined those who may confer or delegate confessional jurisdiction and cardinals are not included among those listed.[10] There is, therefore, in the law as contained in canons 874 and 875 an *implicit* prohibition against cardinals delegating their ordinary confessional jurisdiction, and the clause of canon 199, § 1 *"nisi aliud expresse iure caveatur"* is verified with regard to the ordinary jurisdiction of cardinals.[11]

Authors who claim that cardinals are an exception to the gen-

[7] It is to be remembered that cardinals are here being considered merely *as cardinals.* If a cardinal is also a residential bishop, then as a bishop he can delegate jurisdiction within his territory. Cf. canons 873, 874.

[8] Canon 199, § 1: Qui iurisdictionis potestatem habet ordinariam, potest eam alteri ex tota vel ex parte delegare, nisi aliud expresse iure caveatur.

[9] Cf. Blat, *Commentarium,* II, n. 148.

[10] The Code Commission in a response dated October 16, 1919 (*AAS,* XI [1919], 477; Bouscaren, *Digest,* I, 410). declared that pastors could not delegate their ordinary confessional jurisdiction. Like the cardinals no mention of pastors is made in canons 874 and 875. Therefore, it may be concluded that cardinals, like pastors, are *implicitly* prohibited to delegate their ordinary confessional jurisdiction.

[11] Cf. Blat, *Commentarium,* III, Pars I, n. 196, p. 219; Coronata, *Institutiones,* I (1928), n. 288, p. 330, note 5; Cocchi, *Commentarium,* II (1937), n. 120; Cappello, *Tractatus Canonico-Moralis de Sacramentis* (3 vols. in 6), Vol. II, Pars. I: *De Poenitentia,* Romae: Marietti (1928), II, n. 388; Sipos, *Enchiridion Iuris Canonici* (3. ed., Pecs, 1936), p. 170 (henceforth cited as *Enchiridion*); Vermeersch-Creusen, *Epitome,* II (5. ed., 1934), n. 147.

eral rule of delegating ordinary jurisdiction as contained in Canon 199, § 1, seem to do so in view of the fact that there is no *explicit* prohibition against such delegation.[12]

Another argument against the delegation of this jurisdiction can be taken from the second section of canon 239, § 1. There it is stated that the confessor chosen by a cardinal for himself and his household acquires jurisdiction from the law itself (*ipso iure*) if he lacks it. Were the cardinal able to delegate his ordinary power, it would be sufficient that he invite a priest to hear the confessions of himself and his household, without the need of a special delegation *a iure* to make the priest competent.[13] Moreover, it would be foolish to refer to this power of electing a confessor as *a privilege* if the cardinal could delegate his ordinary jurisdiction.[14]

Section 2. The Extensive Faculties of Cardinals Enjoyed By Way of Privilege

Although cardinals by virtue of Canon 873, § 1 have ordinary jurisdiction for hearing confessions, by Canon 239, § 1, n. 1 they are *privileged* to exercise it without many of the territorial and personal limitations that the common law generally places even on ordinary jurisdiction.[15]

A. Cardinals Are Not Restricted to Certain Territories or to Subjects

The general law states that judicial jurisdiction, whether ordinary or delegated, can be exercised only within one's territory.[16]

[12] Cf. Maroto, *Institutiones*, I, p. 845, nota 2; Kearney, *Principles of Delegation*, p. 77.

[13] Cf. Kearney, *Principles of Delegation*, p. 78.

[14] Cf. Vermeersch-Creusen, *Epitome*, II, n. 147; Maroto, *Institutiones*, I, p. 845, nota 2.

[15] It is to be remembered that the ordinary jurisdiction spoken of in canons 873, § 1 and 239, § 1, n. 1 regards only the *internal sacramental* forum. Cardinals, especially with regard to the absolution from censures, have no jurisdiction through this privilege in either the external forum or the internal nonsacramental forum. (Cf. canon 196.)

[16] Canon 201, § 2.

This means that within the territory of one's jurisdiction he can hear the confessions of both subjects and non-subjects.[17] An exception is made for all those who possess *ordinary* confessional jurisdiction. They can hear the confessions *of their subjects* anywhere in the world.[18]

To these limitations placed on confessional jurisdiction cardinals are not subject, for they can hear the confessions *of anyone, anywhere in the world.*

B. Cardinals Are Not Subject to the Common Law Regulations Regarding Jurisdiction for Hearing Confessions of Men and Women Religious

(*a*) *Cardinals Enjoy Faculties For All Male Religious*

This privilege gives cardinals faculties to hear the confessions of *all religious*. This includes religious men whether clerical or lay, exempt or non-exempt, together with religious women, whether *sorores* or *moniales*.

With regard to *clerical exempt men* this is fittingly called a privilege, for the general law states that to hear validly the confessions of such religious, delegation must be obtained either from the religious superior or the Ordinary of the place where the confessions are to be heard.[19] Cardinals, however, without the necessity of jurisdiction or approbation from the local Ordinary or religious superior can validly and licitly hear the confessions of any exempt clerical religious in any place. They may also, as will be seen

[17] Canon 881, § 1.

[18] Canons 201, § 2; 881, § 2.

[19] Cf. canons 874, § 1; 875; 518; 519. Prior to 1913, any regular who confessed to a priest not designated by the superior, confessed not only illicitly but invalidly. The Sacred Congregation of Religious in a decree approved by Pius X on August 5, 1913 (nn. 1, 14, 15—*AAS,* V [1913], 431), abrogated this strict regulation so that a regular might confess to any priest approved by the local ordinary. His legislation is today expressed in canon 519. Cf. Gomez, "De Regularium Confessionibus"—*Commentarium pro Religiosis* (Romae, 1920—), VIII (1927), 369; McCormick, *Confessors of Religious,* The Catholic University of America Canon Law Studies, n. 33 (Washington, D. C.: The Catholic University of America, 1926), pp. 29-30.

below, absolve from any sin or censure reserved in a clerical exempt Order or Congregation.[20]

In the case both of *clerics who are not exempt* as well as lay *religious men who are exempt* the general law states that the confessors are to be proposed by the superior to the local Ordinary who is to grant the necessary jurisdiction.[21] Where *lay religious men who are not exempt* are concerned, the confessor receives his jurisdiction from the local Ordinary.[22]

Cardinals are subject to none of these special regulations. They may hear the confessions of any of these religious anywhere in the world.[23]

(*b*) *Cardinals Enjoy Faculties Also For All Female Religious*

"Every contrary particular law or privilege being revoked, *all priests* whether secular or regular, no matter what may be their dignity or office, must have *special jurisdiction* to hear validly and licitly the confessions of any religious women and novices, *safeguarding, however, the prescription of canons 239, § 1, n. 1, 522 and 523.* This jurisdiction is to be conferred by the Ordinary of the place in which the house of the religious is situated." [24]

In view of this canon which directly regards the *ordinary* or *extraordinary* and *supplementary* confessor of religious women,[25] no other priest, *with the exception of a cardinal,* can validly hear the confessions of any women religious, whether *sorores* or *moniales,*

[20] Cf. canons 896 and 2220, § 1.

[21] Cf. canons 874, 875, § 2, 518, 519; Creusen, *Religious Men and Women in the Code* (Translated from the French by Edward F. Garesché, S.J.; fourth English edition revised and edited to conform with the fifth French edition by Adam C. Ellis, S.J., Milwaukee: Bruce, 1942), n. 105.

[22] Cf. canons 528, 529.

[23] It is to be remembered that the limitations mentioned govern the faculties of the *Ordinary* confessor of Religious men. Exceptions whereby male religious may confess to any priest approved by the local Ordinary are mentioned in canon 519.

[24] Canon 876, §§ 1 and 2; cf. McCormick, *Confessors of Religious,* pp. 100-108.

[25] Cf. canons 520, 521.

or novices unless he has received from the local ordinary at least the jurisdiction for hearing the confessions of women.[26] Even in such a case, since such a priest has no *special jurisdiction* for women religious, it is required for the *validity* of his absolution that the confession be made only in a place approved for hearing the confessions of women.[27]

Cardinals by virtue of canon 239, § 1, n. 1 are exempt from these restrictions governing the confessions of Religious women. They are privileged to hear the confession of any woman religious, novice or postulant throughout the world. The validity of their absolution is never affected by their hearing the confession in a place not approved for hearing the confessions of women, as it is for the confessor of canon 522. Since cardinals enjoy by reason of canon 239 the *special jurisdiction* mentioned in canon 876, § 1, the regulations governing the place in which such confessions are to be heard, affect only the *licitness* of a cardinal's absolution.[28]

C. Cardinals Can Validly and Licitly Absolve From Most of the Reserved Sins and Censures

Confessional jurisdiction is limited in most cases either by the common law or particular law with regard to the types of sins and censures that may be absolved. In danger of death, however, such restrictions do not apply and any priest, even if he has received no jurisdiction or has been excommunicated or suspended, may then validly absolve from all sins and censures no matter how reserved or notorious.[29] Cardinals, however, are privileged to absolve in the ordinary cases outside the danger of death from most reserved sins and censures.

[26] Cf. canon 522.

[27] Cf. canons 522, 909, 910, § 1, together with two responses of the Code Commission: *AAS,* XII (1920), 575; XXVII (1935), 92; Bouscaren, *Digest,* I (1934), 295 and II (1943), 161.

[28] Cf. Vermeersch-Creusen, *Epitome,* II, n. 197; DeSobradillo, *De Religiosarum Confessariis* (Torino: R. Berutti & Co., 1932), p. 137 cum nota (1) ad calcem; McCormick, *Confessors of Religious,* pp. 207-213, 245.

[29] Canon 882.

(a) *Cardinal's Jurisdiction Does Not Extend to Sin of Complicity*

The first restriction regarding the type of sin that may be validly absolved in the ordinary case *extra periculum mortis* is had in the sin of complicity (*absolutio complicis*). No priest, no matter how great his jurisdiction or dignity, can validly absolve his accomplice from the sin of complicity *extra periculum mortis*.[80]

Although the case is difficult to envisage because of the moral qualities requisite before one be promoted to the cardinalate, nevertheless since all are human, should a cardinal be guilty of such a sin, he would have no jurisdiction over his accomplice, and any attempted absolution would consequently be invalid.[81] This is evident firstly from the very nature of the matter concerned and from the end that the legislator had in mind, namely, that confessions of this kind might not be the occasion of a penitent's spiritual ruination.[82] Moreover, Pope Benedict XIV withdrew jurisdiction in such cases from all priest-accomplices *regardless of their dignity or any special privileges or indults they may possess*.[83] Finally, this is evident from the fact that canon 884 speaks not of the confessor but of the *absolution* that is attempted by the confessor.[84] It refers, therefore, *to anyone* who has confessional jurisdiction whether ordinary or delegated.

Should a cardinal attempt to absolve his accomplice, his absolution would be certainly invalid, but he would not incur the *latae sententiae* censure of excommunication most specially reserved to the Holy See by which such a delict is ordinarily punished.[85] The reason for this is that cardinals are not specifically mentioned in canon 2367, § 1, and unless specifically mentioned they are not subject to the penal laws of the Code.[86]

[80] Canon 884, together with the Constitution of Benedict XIV, "*Sacramentum Poenitentiae*," 1 iun., 1741, § 4—*Codex Iuris Canonici*, Documentum V.

[81] Cf. Linahen, *De Absolutione Complicis in Peccato Turpi*, The Catholic University of America Canon Law Studies, n. 164 (Washington, D. C.: The Catholic University of America Press, 1942), p. 36.

[82] Const., "*Sacramentum Poenitentiae*," § 4.

[83] *Ibid.*

[84] "*Absolutio* complicis in peccato turpi invalida est. . . ."

[85] Canon 2367, § 1.

[86] Canon 2227, § 2.

(*b*) *Cardinal's Jurisdiction Extends to All Other Sins Even Though Reserved*

With the single exception mentioned above, cardinals can validly and licitly absolve from all other sins no matter how reserved.[37]

Reservation of sin implies a limitation of jurisdiction. By it a superior draws such a sin to his own tribunal thereby limiting the power of absolution of his inferiors. Since it is a restriction of jurisdiction, it is not a punishment and therefore directly affects the confessor and only indirectly the penitent. The Holy See, by a general law, can thus limit the jurisdiction of all confessors.[38] At present, there is only one such case. That is the case of a false accusation by which an innocent priest is accused before ecclesiastical judges of the crime of solicitation.[39]

Cardinals by reason of their extensive faculties granted in canon 239, § 1, n. 1 are privileged to absolve from this sin reserved to the Holy See, for the canon in granting them faculties over reserved sins makes no distinction.[40] But in so doing, they must observe the conditions mentioned in canon 2363, namely, they shall not absolve from it unless the penitent shall have formally retracted the false denunciation and shall have repaired as far as possible any damage that may have resulted therefrom. Moreover, a grave and protracted penance is to be imposed.[41]

Many other sins may be reserved by local Ordinaries for their dioceses or by the competent clerical religious superior for his subjects.[42] In so doing, the local Ordinary or competent religious

[37] A sin may be reserved *ratione sui* or *ratione censurae*. Only those reserved *ratione sui* are concerned here. Sins reserved *ratione censurae* will be treated in the section on the cardinals' faculty to absolve from reserved censures.

[38] Cf. canon 893.

[39] Canon 894. By virtue of canon 2363 this sin is also reserved to the Holy See *ratione censurae*.

[40] Cf. Toso, *Commentaria*, II, tom. II, p. 35.

[41] That cardinals must observe these conditions is evident by way of analogy from the fact that other confessors who give absolution from this sin by virtue of *special* faculties are bound to observe them. Cf. *AAS*, XXI (1929), 12, n. 4, a; XXVI (1934), 149, n. VII; Bouscaren, *Digest*, I (1934), 589, 874.

[42] Cf. canons 893, § 1; 896.

superior limits the jurisdiction of confessors who have jurisdiction to hear confessions within that territory. Since cardinals are privileged to hear the confessions of any person, lay or religious, in any part of the world without the need of delegation or approbation, and since canon 239, § 1, n. 1 gives them faculties over reserved sins without exception, they are not subject to the territorial limitations of jurisdiction that bishops or religious superiors might impose. They can, therefore, absolve within the confines of any local Ordinary's jurisdiction any penitent confessing a sin that the Ordinary in question has reserved to himself. They may act similarly with regard to sins reserved in any clerical exempt Order or Community.

(c) *This Ordinary Confessional Jurisdiction of Cardinals Extends Also to Most of the Reserved Censures*

Because of the dignity that the cardinals enjoy in the universal Church the legislator has seen fit to extend by way of privilege the confessional jurisdiction of cardinals not only to reserved sins but also to almost every censure even though reserved.

Censures [43] are variously divided in the Code. They may be decreed either *a iure* or *ab homine.* An *a iure* censure is one that is contained in the law itself. An *ab homine* censure is one that, although prescribed by the law, is inflicted through particular precept of the superior or through the condemnatory sentence of a judge.[44]

Censures may be either *latae sententiae* or *ferendae sententiae.* A *latae sententiae* censure is one that is incurred by the very fact that one commits the delict to which it is attached. A *ferendae sententiae* censure is one that must be inflicted by a superior or a judge. After the condemnatory sentence has been passed, these latter censures are considered as *ab homine* censures.[45]

Of these various censures some are *reserved* while others are *not reserved.*[46] An *ab homine* censure according to the general law is

[43] Cf. canon 2241.
[44] Cf. canon 2217, § 1, n. 3.
[45] Cf. canon 2217, § 1, nn. 2, 3.
[46] Canon 2245, § 1.

reserved at all times and in all places to the one who inflicted the censure or passed the sentence, or to his competent superior, successor or delegate.[47] A *latae sententiae* censure is never reserved unless in the law or precept it is expressly said to be reserved. When there is a doubt it is to be considered as not reserved.[48] An *a iure* censure *of particular law* may be reserved by the bishop to himself or by the competent religious superior to himself. But such reservations have value only within the territory of their jurisdiction.[49] An *a iure* censure *of the general law* when reserved, is reserved sometimes to the local Ordinary and sometimes to the Holy See.[50] Of those reserved to the Holy See, some are reserved *simpliciter*, others *speciali modo* and still others *specialissimo modo*.[51]

Any censure once incurred can be removed only by legitimate absolution,[52] either in the external or internal forum.[53] It is in this regard that the cardinals' privilege is to be considered. Again, only the ordinary case outside the danger of death is contemplated, for *in periculo mortis* and *in casibus urgentioribus* special faculties are granted *a iure*.[54]

Firstly, it is to be noted that this privilege of cardinals does not extend to vindicative penalties since they are not mentioned in the canon. Moreover, this jurisdiction of cardinals over censures applies only to the *internal sacramental forum*. This is evident from the fact that canons 873 and 239, § 1, n. 1 are dealing exclusively with confessional jurisdiction and also from the fact that cardinals as such have no jurisdiction in the external forum. This has some very important practical consequences. Censures are punishments of the

[47] Cf. canons 2245, § 1; 2247, § 2.

[48] Canon 2245, § 4.

[49] Canons 893, 2246, § 1 and 2247, §§ 1 and 2.

[50] Canon 2245, § 2.

[51] Canon 2245, § 3. For a further treatment of the reservation of censures, cf. Stadalnikas, *Reservation of Censures*, The Catholic University of America Canon Law Studies, n. 208 (Washington, D. C.: The Catholic University of America Press, 1944).

[52] Canon 2248, § 1.

[53] Cf. canons 2250, 2251.

[54] Cf. canons 882, 2252 and 2254.

external forum,[55] depriving one of the benefits which the christian possesses as a member of the christian society rather than as an individual. Consequently absolution from censures is *regularly an act of external administration,* giving back the lost advantages of membership in the church. Absolution in the external forum completely removes all the effects of censures and affects the internal as well as the external forum. One absolved *in the internal forum,* as would be the case when a cardinal uses the special faculties he enjoys by way of privilege, is really absolved before God, but the absolution is supposed to be unknown. For the Church or the public it is as if it had not been received. Hence, if the censure remains occult, the person thus absolved becomes free from all restriction. If, however, the censure was public or notorious, in the eyes of the community, it continues to be binding and should be respected when acting; otherwise, *scandal* is likely to be caused. Thus, for instance, if a cardinal in the internal sacramental forum absolved a penitent from a censure incurred by reason of a public delict, the penitent, unless some proof of the absolution could be had or legitimately presumed in the external forum, cannot perform any acts in the external forum that are likely to cause scandal. Consequently, if scandal would be caused if such a penitent, publicly considered to be still under censure, should receive Communion, he would have to refrain from receiving It.[56] But nothing would prevent such a penitent from going to some other place where he is not known to receive Communion there. If there is no danger of scandal, one absolved in the internal forum may act in the external forum as if he had obtained full release.[57]

From the wording of this privilege as contained in the law, cardinals may validly absolve in the sacramental forum from *all censures* no matter how reserved, *excepting only* censures that are reserved to

[55] Cf. canon 2195, § 1.

[56] Cf. Sole, *De Delictis et Poenis* (Romae: Pustet, 1920), n. 185; also the private response on this matter by the S.C.C., 18 nov. 1922, as reported in Bouscaren, *Digest,* I, 408-409.

[57] Cf. Canon 2251 and Ayrinhac, *Penal Legislation in the New Code of Canon Law* (Revised by Rev. P. J. Lydon, New York: Benziger Brothers, 1936), n. 92.

the Holy See *specialissimo modo* and those annexed to the breaking of the oath of secrecy of the Holy Office.

Cardinals, therefore, may absolve from *non-reserved censures,* since every confessor enjoys this faculty.[58] They may also absolve from censures *reserved a iure,* whether in particular or general law.[59] This includes those that are *reserved by the general law to the local Ordinary,*[60] as well as those reserved *to the Holy See either simpliciter or speciali modo.*[61]

Canon 2253 n. 3 which treats of those who may absolve from censures reserved *a iure,* enunciates the general law and therefore does not include cardinals. The reason for such an omission is that cardinals are an exception to the general law since they enjoy their faculty by way of privilege.[62]

The only doubt that might arise is had regarding *ab homine* censures. The general law states that these are always and everywhere reserved to the one who inflicted the censure or passed the sentence, or to his competent superior, successor or delegate,[63] and that they alone can grant legitimate absolution *extra periculum mortis.*[64]

The above is the general law. Cardinals, however, are conceded a *privilege contained within the common law,* and therefore, the interpretation of such a privilege, like that of all privileges, is to be taken from the wording of the privilege itself.[65] In the privilege itself it is stipulated that cardinals may absolve in the sacramental forum *"ubique terrarum"* from *all* sins and censures, even if they be reserved, excepting *only* (*"exceptis tantum"*) those reserved *specialissimo modo* to the Holy See and those incurred by violating the secret of the Holy Office. Since the legislator used the words

[58] Canon 2253, n. 1.

[59] Cf. Cappello, *De Sacramentis,* II, Pars I: *De Poenitentia,* n. 572.

[60] Cf. for example, canons 2319, 2350.

[61] Cf. for example, canons 2335, 2338, 2341, 2343.

[62] The more general canon 2236, § 1 can be said to include cardinals since it uses the phrase *"ab eo cui haec potestas commissa est."*

[63] Canons 2245, § 2, 2247, § 2.

[64] Canon 2253, n. 2.

[65] Canon 67: Privilegium ex ipsius tenore aestimandum est, nec licet illud extendere aut restringere.

"exceptis tantum," it is not permitted, in accordance with the rule for interpreting privileges, to restrict this faculty by excepting from it censures other than those that the legislator himself has excepted.

Among post-Code commentators, there does not seem to be sufficient clarity in this matter. The majority, in treating canon 239, § 1, n. 1, merely quote the canon, thereby implying that the only exceptions to be made are those that are explicitly included in the canon. Coronata, however, excludes, although timorously, *ad homine* censures from the scope of the cardinals' faculty.[66]

The issue becomes confused, however, when one consults the authors who, in their commentaries on Book V of the Code, treat of those who may legitimately absolve from censures in the ordinary cases *extra periculum mortis*. Some of these authors merely quote Canon 2253 and make no mention of cardinals at all.[67] Cipollini,[68] Cappello,[69] Cocchi [70] and Beste [71] mention cardinals among those who may absolve from *a iure* reserved censures but fail to mention them among those who may absolve from *ab homine* censures. Since cardinals are not mentioned by the Code either among those who may absolve from *a iure* reserved censures,[72] or among those who may absolve from *ab homine* censures,[73] it would seem that these latter authors do not extend a cardinal's jurisdiction to *ab homine* censures. Hence, the confusion.

The writer, in view of the following arguments, is of the opinion that it is at the very least solidly probable that cardinals may absolve from *ab homine* censures.

[66] *Institutiones,* I, n. 325, p. 381, nota (5) ad calcem: "In hac facultate videntur solummodo comprehendi censurae a iure, non ab homine." It is to be noted that he uses the word *"videntur."*

[67] E. g., Ayrinhac, Blat, Coronata, Sole and Vermeersch-Creusen.

[68] *De Censuris Latae Sententiae iuxta Codicem Iuris Canonici* (Taurini: Marietti, 1925), nn. 41-44.

[69] *Tractatus Canonico Moralis de Censuris* (Taurinorum Augustae: Marietti, 1925), n. 121.

[70] *Commentarium,* V (4. ed., Taurinorum Augustae: Marietti, 1938), n. 77.

[71] *Introductio in Codicem,* p. 910.

[72] Canon 2253, n. 3.

[73] Canon 2253, n. 2.

(a) From the wording of canon 239, § 1, n. 1 which excepts only (*"exceptis tantum"*) those mentioned in it.

(b) By way of analogy from the fact that when the legislator in other canons of the Code meant to except *ab homine* censures, he did so specifically.[74] Coronata uses this argument in relation to canon 2249, § 2 where there is a case similar to that of canon 239, § 1, n. 1.[75]

(c) It is not repugnant to the nature of *ab homine* censures that the faculty to absolve from them is extended to cardinals, for such faculties, explicitly comprehending censures *ab homine* have been granted to simple confessors, e. g. during a Jubilee Year,[76] and simple confessors most certainly are not comprehended under canon 2245, § 2.

(d) Finally, the authors who include cardinals among those who may absolve from *a iure* reserved censures should, to be logical, include them also among those who may absolve from *ab homine* censures, since cardinals are not specifically mentioned by the Code in either case.[77]

D. Censures That Are Excepted From the Cardinals' Faculty

The legislator has excepted from the cardinals' confessional jurisdiction censures that are reserved to the Holy See *"specialissimo modo."* These are incurred (1) by those who throw away the con-

[74] E. g., canons 2247, § 3 and 2252.

[75] *Institutiones,* IV (Taurini: Marietti, 1935), n. 1755, p. 171: "Cum Codex hic c. 2249, § 2 exceptionem tantum ponat de censura specialissimo modo reservata, non de censura reservata *ab homine,* quaeritur utrum ad hanc alteram censuram exceptio sit extendenda. Cum Codex quando agitur de excipienda censura *ab homine* clare id exprimat (cf. cc. 2247, § 3 et 2252), et hic taceat, exceptio restringenda videtur ad censuras specialissimo modo reservatas."

[76] Cf. *AAS,* XVII (1925), 611, n. III; XXVI (1934), 137, n. VIII, 3; Bouscaren, *Digest,* I, 858, 869-870.

[77] The fact that they are not mentioned in canon 2253, nn. 2, 3, or 2245, § 2 can be explained inasmuch as these canons express the general law. The cardinals' faculty is granted them by way of privilege and is therefore an exception to the general law. Cardinals can be said to be implicitly mentioned in the phrase *"ab eo cui haec potestas commissa est"* of the more general canon 2236, § 1.

secrated Hosts or carry them off or keep them for an evil purpose; [78] (2) by those who lay violent hands on the person of the Roman Pontiff; [79] (3) by those confessors who absolve or pretend to absolve an accomplice in *peccato turpi*,[80] and (4) by those confessors who *directly* violate the seal of confession.[81]

To these may be added those censures contained in the Constitution of Pius X, *Vacante Sede Apostolica,* 25 dec. 1904, which governs papal elections.[82] These censures are more than *specialissimo modo reservatae,* for they are reserved *personally* to the Roman Pontiff and only *"in articulo mortis"* can they be absolved by any other, regardless of any faculty he may possess.[83] They are therefore excluded from the cardinals' faculty.

Another that may be added to these is the censure incurred by a priest who has attempted marriage and who, for grave reasons, cannot leave his "wife." Ordinarily, the censure of a priest who attempts marriage is excommunication *simpliciter* reserved to the Holy See.[84] Where, however, because of grave reasons separation is impossible and the priest has repented and seeks to be admitted to the reception of the sacraments after the manner of a layman, promising to observe absolute and perfect chastity forever in the future, absolution is reserved *exclusively* to the Sacred Penitentiary. It is so reserved to the Sacred Penitentiary (by two decrees, one dated April 18, 1936,[85] the other of May 3, 1937 [86] that "no one, except in the case of danger of death, can ever absolve from it, notwithstanding any faculty granted either by canon 2254, § 1, or by privilege, or finally by any other law whatsoever."

The final exception stated in Canon 239, § 1, n. 1 is that of censures that bind those who violate the oath of secrecy of the Holy Office. Not only the cardinals and officials who pertain to the

[78] Canon 2320.

[79] Canon 2343, § 1, n. 1.

[80] Canon 2367.

[81] Canon 2369, § 1.

[82] Cf. *Codex Iuris Canonici,* Docum. I, nn. 37, 51, 52, 69, 79, 80, 81 and 82.

[83] Const. *Vacante Sede Apostolica,* n. 51.

[84] Canon 2388, § 1.

[85] *AAS,* XXVIII (1936), 242; Bouscaren, *Digest,* II, 579-580.

[86] *AAS,* XXIX (1937), 283; Bouscaren, *Digest,* II, 580-581.

Congregation of the Holy Office are bound by this secret, but also anyone who is engaged in certain affairs pertaining to the Sacred Consistorial Congregation, together with all officials who are concerned in the processes of beatification and canonization handled by the Congregation of Rites. Absolution from the censure incurred by violating this secret must always be sought from the Sacred Penitentiary.[87] Cardinals, therefore, may not absolve from such censures.

Section 3. Cardinals' Obligation to Make Use of These Faculties

As has been stated the cardinalitial privileges contained in the Code are *strict* privileges, i. e. the grantee may use or neglect the use of his privileges.[88] The privilege here in question, however, is one that from its very nature is granted more for the benefit of others than as a favor solely for the benefit of the cardinals. Therefore, even if one would interpret the cardinalitial privileges, which are *privilegia legis*, as *privileges*, rather than more properly *as laws*, canon 69 would not apply.[89] Moreover, even if it could be considered as a privilege granted in favor of cardinals alone, there is an obligation to use it arising from another source, namely the common good or possible private injury.

Because it is granted with the benefit of others in view, cardinals are obliged to use it whenever approached in that regard.[90] A penitent approaching any priest and asking to have his confession heard can be presumed to be in serious need. *A fortiori* in view of the high dignity of the cardinalate, a penitent approaching a cardinal can be presumed to be in very serious need. Therefore, the

[87] Coronata, *Institutiones,* IV (Taurini, 1935), n. 1750, p. 162; Toso, *Commentaria,* Lib. II, Tom. II (Romae, 1923), pp. 35-36; *AAS,* IX (1917), 232, ad IV.

[88] Cf. *above,* p. 2.

[89] Canon 69: "Nemo cogitur uti privilegio in sui dumtaxat favorem concesso, nisi alio ex capite exsurgat obligatio." For a complete treatment of this canon cf. Roelker, *Principles of Privilege,* pp. 93-98; Cicognani, *Canon Law,* pp. 804-805.

[90] Cf. canon 892, § 2; Cicognani, *Canon Law,* p. 804.

cardinal would be obliged *ex caritate* to hear the confession,[91] and if the penitent confesses reserved sins or censures over which the cardinal has faculties, the cardinal would be obliged to use his privilege and absolve the penitent.[92]

If a cardinal refused to make use of his faculty, definite spiritual harm would result for the penitent, since he would be forced to remain in sin or censure, whereas the cardinal with the proper intention and the use of the ordinary form of absolution as contained in the Ritual[93] could absolve him from both sin and censure. It can therefore be concluded that the use of this privilege is obligatory.

Article II. Privilege of Choosing Any Priest As Confessor

Canon 239, § 1, n. 2. Sibi suisque familiaribus eligendi sacerdotem confessionibus excipiendis, qui, si iurisdictione careat, eam ipso iure obtinet, etiam quod spectat ad peccata et censuras, reservatas quoque, illis tantum censuris exceptis, de quibus in n. 1.

By this section of Canon 239 cardinals are privileged to choose any priest as confessor for themselves and the members of their household. Should this priest not have jurisdiction, he obtains it *ipso iure* by his choice as confessor, and this jurisdiction conferred by the law itself includes the same faculty to absolve from reserved sins and censures that the cardinal himself enjoys.[94]

Far from being new, this privilege was granted long before the

[91] *Loc. cit.*

[92] It is to be presupposed that the penitent has the proper contrition and dispositions necessary for absolution (cf. c. 2242, § 3). The cardinal, moreover, in order to safeguard the efficacy of censure and reservation should impose the obligations that would ordinarily be imposed by the superior to whom under the general law the sin or censure is reserved. These are the reparation of injury done to a third party; the reparation as much as possible of any scandal to which the penitent has given occasion; a canonical penance, over and above the sacramental penance, in accordance with the gravity of the case (cf. cc. 2248, § 2; 2312).

[93] Cf. canon 2250, § 3.

[94] This privilege is also enjoyed by both residential and titular bishops. (Canon 349, § 1, n. 1.)

present Code. Its basis is a decree of Gregory IX promulgated between the years 1227 and 1234.[95] Gregory granted the privilege to bishops and *"aliis superioribus."* That cardinals were comprehended under this latter phrase was unanimously held by the commentators.[96]

Subsequent to the Council of Trent this confessor had to be one who was approved by the local Ordinary.[97] The Code, however, has abrogated this requirement by stating that if a priest selected as a confessor by a cardinal lacks jurisdiction, he automatically by the very fact of his selection receives the necessary jurisdiction *a iure.* Thus the local Ordinary's approbation is no longer *a conditio sine qua non.*

Cardinals may use and enjoy this privilege everywhere, as often as they wish, without any limitation concerning the quality or number of priests so selected. Moreover, this selection may be made by a cardinal either for an indefinite period of time, a definite period of time or even for a single particular case.[98]

That this is truly a privilege is evident from the stipulations of the common law. Were it not for this privilege, a priest selected by a cardinal as his confessor would be subject to the limitations placed on confessional jurisdiction by the common law, whether that jurisdiction be ordinary and thus limited to one's subjects[99] or delegated and therefore territorially limited.[100]

[95] C. 16, X, *de poenitentiis et remissionibus,* V, 38: "Ne pro dilatione poenitentiae periculum immineat animarum, permittimus episcopis et aliis superioribus, nec non minoribus praelatis exemptis ut etiam praeter sui superioris licentiam providum et discretum sibi possint eligere confessorem." (1227-1234,—Potthast, *Regista Pontificum Romanorum inde ab A. post Christum Natum 1198 ad A. 1304* [2 vols., Berolini, 1874-1875], n. 9685. Henceforth cited as Potthast.)

[96] Cf. Diana, *Resolutiones Morales,* Vol. 5, tom. 9, tract. 7: *De Potestate et Privilegiis S.R.E. Cardinalium,* res. 36; Fagnanus, *Commentaria,* in c. 16, X, *de poenitentiis et remissionibus,* V, 38, n. 31; Barbosa, *Iuris ecclesiastici universi libri III,* Vol. I, cap. IV, n. 78.

[97] Cf. Conc. Trident., sess. XXIII, *de ref.,* cap. 15—Schroeder, *Canons and Decrees of the Council of Trent,* p. 173; Fagnanus, *loc. cit.*

[98] Cf. Berutti, *in Jus Pontificum* (Romae, 1921—), XIV (1934), 57 sq.

[99] Cf. canons 201, § 2 and 881, § 2.

[100] Cf. canons 201, § 2 and 881, § 1.

Besides removing such limitations, the legislator has gone much farther in removing the other general limitations arising from the reservation of sins and censures, so that a priest thus selected enjoys in absolving the cardinal and the members of his household the same powers that the cardinal himself enjoys when acting as confessor.

It should be noted that these faculties actively enjoyed by a priest so selected, though identical with those the cardinal himself enjoys, are not delegated to the priest by the cardinal, for it has already been seen that a cardinal cannot delegate the powers he enjoys by way of privilege. These faculties come to the priest *a iure.* The act by which a priest is petitioned to hear the cardinal's confession is merely the occasion of this *a iure* delegation.

The faculties thus conferred by the law on such a priest can be passively enjoyed not only by the cardinal but also by the members of his household. However, not every confessor to whom the *familiares* confess receives this power, but only he who is selected by the cardinal as the confessor for his household. The *familiares* cannot make the selection, it must be made by the cardinal himself who must make it clear that he intends or consents to have the members of his household make their confessions to this priest.[101]

The canon uses the words *"suis familiaribus."* The term *familiares* does not include everyone who might be staying in the cardinal's home. The canonical notion of *familiaris* indicates a person, whether lay, cleric or religious, who is in the cardinal's employ *per modum habitus,* receiving for his or her services a fixed salary, and who, moreover, *permanently* dwells in the cardinal's home or on the grounds thereof.[102] In other words, the members of the cardinal's household include his secretary and servants, e. g. the housekeeper, cook, chauffeur, gardener, etc. All of these to confess to the priest selected must live in the cardinal's home or on the grounds thereof, e. g. in the servants' quarters. The home might be cared for by Sisters. In that case, such religious women could make use of this confessor's ample faculties.[103]

Those who are not considered *"familiares"* and who therefore can-

[101] Cf. Berutti, *loc. cit.*

[102] Cf. Toso, *Commentaria,* lib. II, tom. II, p. 36; Berutti, *loc. cit.*

[103] Cf. De Sobradillo, *De Religiosarum Confessariis,* p. 237.

not make use of this confessor would be e. g., relatives living with the cardinal, or friends staying with the cardinal as guests.

A question arises as to whether a cardinal could select a priest who is under a censure of excommunication or suspension *post sententiam*. Ordinarily, the absolutions given by such a priest are invalid, except in the case of a penitent being in danger of death.[104]

The solution of this question depends on the interpretation of the phrase "*si iurisdictione careat*" of this section of canon 239. It could conceivably refer to a priest who had never received confessional jurisdiction from the Ordinary of the place in which the cardinal happens to be when he seeks a priest confessor. On the other hand, it could also refer to a priest who had received jurisdiction, which jurisdiction, however, had been suspended by the *post sententiam* censure.

Canon 2264 seems to exclude the possibility of a cardinal's choosing such a priest, for it states that any jurisdictional act placed by such a censured priest is null, except when a penitent is *in periculo mortis*. The fact that special jurisdiction is conferred on him *a iure* by the fact of the cardinal's selecting him would seem to be of no consequence, since the censure rules out all jurisdictional acts regardless of the source of the jurisdiction.

On the other hand, we are here concerned with a privilege; a favorable exception from the general law. Therefore, if one takes the phrase "*si iurisdictione careat*" as it stands in canon 239, § 1, n. 2, it would seem to include such a priest, for a priest under a *post sententiam* censure of excommunication or suspension certainly *lacks* the necessary jurisdiction to hear confessions. The fact that the cardinal elects him as confessor confers on him new jurisdiction which has as its source the law itself, making it analogous to that conferred by canon 882. The effects of the censure would therefore seem not to bind and his absolution would be valid.

In view of the arguments given above, both opinions seem probable. A *dubium iuris*, therefore, arises, and if a cardinal were to elect such a priest as his confessor, the absolutions granted would, in virtue of canon 209, be valid.

There is a simpler and more practical solution of this problem

[104] Cf. canons 2261, § 3; 2264; 2284.

that excludes any doubt. Should such a case arise, the cardinal could first, by virtue of his own extensive faculties, hear the priest's confession and provided the required dispositions are present and the censure is one over which the cardinal has faculties, absolve the priest from the censure. The obstacle that might otherwise prevent the priest from placing jurisdictional acts is thereby removed and the cardinal could then select him as confessor for himself and his household.

Article III. Privilege of Administering the Sacrament of Confirmation

Canon 239, § 1, n. 23. Ministrandi sacramentum confirmationis, firmo onere inscriptionis nominis confirmati ad normam iuris.

Canon 782, § 2. Extraordinarius minister (confirmationis) est presbyter cui vel iure communi vel peculiari Sedis Apostolicae indulto ea facultas concessa sit.

Canon 782, § 3. Hac facultate ipso iure gaudent, praeter S.R.E. Cardinales ad normam canon 239, § 1, n. 23, Abbas vel Praelatus nullius, Vicarius et Praefectus Apostolicus, qui tamen ea valide uti nequeunt, nisi intra fines sui territorii et durante munere tantum.

Another privilege that cardinals enjoy with regard to the Sacraments is that of administering the sacrament of Confirmation anywhere in the world. It naturally concerns cardinals who lack the episcopal character, since for a bishop it is not a privilege but a right and duty.[105]

This privilege is new with the Code and by it cardinals are constituted as *extraordinary* ministers of the sacrament since they receive the faculty from the common law.[106]

The extraordinary minister of confirmation, may be defined as "a priest who by divine law does not derive the power to be a minister from the order he has received, but who by the plenitude of power of

[105] Cf. canons 782, 783 and 784.

[106] Canon 782, § 3.

the Roman Pontiff is delegated to administer confirmation." [107] The person to whom the delegation of the Holy See is given must be a priest, because the administration of the sacrament of Confirmation demands essentially an exercise of the sacerdotal order.[108] A deacon could not be delegated to administer confirmation. Just as the Pope cannot give a cleric in minor orders the faculty to absolve from sin, so also he cannot give a deacon or any other one except a priest the power to confirm.[109]

An interesting question arises as to the nature of this power to confirm that is conferred, by way of privilege, on cardinals who lack the episcopal character. It cannot be jurisdiction, for jurisdiction is not at all necessary for the valid administration of Confirmation.[110] Nor can the cardinals receive by delegation *potestas ordinis iuris divini,* since Confirmation is one of the seven Sacraments which were instituted directly by Christ.[111]

Just what is received by the apostolic delegation which enables a simple priest to administer Confirmation, has long been disputed. The writer is inclined to follow Coleman, who gives a complete treatment of this disputed point in his discussion of the extraordinary minister of Confirmation.[112]

Since cardinals who lack the episcopal character do not receive a delegation of jurisdiction or orders, it necessarily must be something else that permits them to administer Confirmation validly. Though, in such a case, the cardinal does not receive a delegation of the power

[107] Cf. Coleman, *The Minister of Confirmation,* The Catholic University of America Canon Law Studies, n. 125 (Washington, D. C.: The Catholic University of America Press, 1941), p. 104.

[108] Coleman, *op. cit.,* p. 108.

[109] Coleman, *op. cit.,* p. 104.

[110] Lehmkuhl, *Theologia Moralis* (2 vols., 10. ed., Friburgi Brisgoviae, 1902), II, n. 134; Diekamp, *Theologiae Dogmaticae Manuale* (2 vols., 6. ed., Parisiis: Declae et Socii, 1934), II, 126; Vermeersch-Creusen, *Epitome,* II, n. 61.

[111] *Potestas ordinis iuris ecclesiastici* may be delegated (canon 210). It will be seen that it is by means of such delegated power that cardinals who lack the episcopal character may confer the non-sacramental orders of Tonsure and Minor Orders.

[112] *Minister of Confirmation,* 106-111.

of orders, it is nevertheless agreed that he confirms by virtue of the power of orders received when he was ordained to the priesthood. That the priesthood is not in itself sufficient for the valid administration of Confirmation, is evident from the practice of the Church and from the fact that Pius X implicitly condemned such an opinion.[113]

Coleman, therefore, concludes that the essential thing that is added to the priesthood by way of delegation is something which belongs to the bishop by reason of his episcopate. By Confirmation a person is constituted a soldier in the spiritual order, just as by the process of military enrollment a man becomes a soldier in the natural order. It is the Chief, the General or the King who admits men to the natural status of soldiers; lower rank officers can do so only with delegated authority. This is true also in ecclesiastical society by way of analogy. It pertains to the bishop as the ecclesiastical chieftain, not by reason of his episcopal order (for otherwise, nobody but a bishop could ever confirm), nor by reason of his jurisdiction (for even after this is taken away he still retains the faculty to confirm), but, *by reason of his ecclesiastical dignity* to constitute soldiers of the spiritual order. The necessary power, therefore, belongs to the bishop because of the preeminence which the episcopate gives him by reason of a *praelatio,* which results from but is not necessarily dependent on the episcopate.[114]

Coleman concludes, then, that when a priest, who is an inferior officer to the bishop in ecclesiastical society, receives the faculty to confirm, he receives "a revocable grant of that dignity or of that preeminence by reason of which the bishop is able to constitute soldiers of Christ. It is not strictly in virtue of this borrowed preeminence that a priest confirms. Rather, this is considered a condition; and given this condition a priest confirms by an exercise of his priestly order."[115]

In view of this opinion, it is this "borrowed preeminence," which, added to his priestly orders, makes a cardinal who lacks the epis-

[113] Ep. *"Ex quo,"* 26 dec. 1910—*AAS,* III (1911), 119.

[114] Coleman, *op. cit.,* 109.

[115] *Op. cit.,* 109-110.

copal character competent to confer the Sacrament of Confirmation validly.

Since the faculty to confirm may be delegated to simple priests,[116] it is altogether fitting that in view of the eminent dignity of the cardinalate, the common law has conceded this faculty to the cardinals. A similar faculty is granted to Abbots or Prelates *nullius* and to Vicars and Prefects Apostolic, but its exercise is limited to their territories. Cardinals are distinguished from these others in that no limitation is placed on them. They may administer Confirmation in any part of the world, even without the permission of the local Ordinary.[117]

The law imposes only one condition for cardinals and that condition is that the confirmation be duly recorded.[118] But the cardinal is not required to do this personally. If the pastor of those confirmed is present at the ceremony, it is his duty without receiving any admonition to make the prescribed entry in the registers.[119] When the pastor has not been present at the confirmation of his subjects, the cardinal is required to inform him or see to it that he is informed about the administration of Confirmation.[120]

[116] Modern instances of such delegation by Apostolic Indult can be found in China and Latin America. It has also been accorded, in particular instances, to chaplains serving with the Armed Forces in the present war. These were only given because of exceptional and pressing circumstances. Cf. *Instructio pro Simplici Sacerdote—AAS,* XXVII (1935), 13. Amongst the Oriental Catholics, confirmation is usually administered to children by a simple priest immediately after baptism. This they do in virtue of a faculty expressly, or at least tacitly, conceded by the Holy See. The Italo-Greek priests do not enjoy such a faculty. Cf. Const. *"Presbyteri Graeci,"* 31 aug. 1595; this constitution of Clement VIII was confirmed by the constitution of Benedict XIV, *"Etsi pastoralis,"* 26 maii 1742. Whether the Oriental Bulgarians enjoy the faculty is a disputed point. Cf. Cappello, *De Sacramentis,* I, n. 842, 3. The Maronites, however, do not confer the Sacrament of Confirmation immediately after baptism as do the other Oriental Disciplines in the case of children. Cf. canon 782, § 5, and Coleman, *op. cit.,* p. 124.

[117] Cf. *Periodica de Re Canonica et Morali* (Brugis, 1905—), XII (1923), (140).

[118] Canon 239, § 1, n. 23.

[119] Cf. canon 798; Coleman, *op. cit.,* p. 119.

[120] Canon 799.

Ordinarily, there is no obligation placed on the cardinal to make use of this privilege, since the faculty of confirming is given him because of his dignity.[121]

ARTICLE IV. PRIVILEGE OF CONFERRING TONSURE AND MINOR ORDERS

Canon 239, § 1, n. 22. Conferendi primam tonsuram et ordines minores, dummodo promovendus habeat dimissorias proprii Ordinarii litteras.

Canon 951. Sacrae ordinationis minister ordinarius est episcopus consecratus; extraordinarius, qui, licet charactere episcopali careat, a iure vel a Sede Apostolica per peculiare indultum potestatem acceperit aliquos ordines conferendi.

The faculty of conferring tonsure and minor orders anywhere in the world is another privilege granted to cardinals who lack the episcopal character. This faculty they enjoyed prior to the Code, but for use in their title churches only.[122]

By this privilege cardinals are constituted as *extraordinary* ministers of ordination.[123] This distinction between the ordinary and extraordinary minister of ordination regards the non-sacramental orders, i. e. tonsure, minor orders and possibly subdiaconate.[124] In other words, the extraordinary minister confers orders not through power he enjoys by reason of ordination and that alone, but through special power received from the Roman Pontiff. The ordinary minister, i. e. a bishop, confers orders through his episcopal power received when he was consecrated.

The power conferred on cardinals by this privilege which regards the conferral of non-sacramental orders, is *potestas ordinis iuris ecclesiastici,* which power is mentioned in canon 210.[125] It is

[121] Blat, *Commentarium,* V. III, Pars I, n. 79.

[122] Cf. *above,* p. 15.

[123] Canon 951.

[124] Cf. Cappello, *De Sacramentis,* Vol. II, Pars III, *De Sacra Ordinatione* (Romae: Marietti, 1935), n. 262.

[125] Canon 210: Potestas ordinis, a legitimo Superiore ecclesiastico sive

apparent from canon 210 that this power granted to cardinals by way of privilege cannot be delegated.

The common law concedes a similar faculty to Vicars and Prefects Apostolic, to Abbots or Prelates *nullius*, who lack the episcopal character.[126] Their faculty, however, is much more limited than that of cardinals, since they are restricted to their own territory (*in proprio territorio*), while cardinals are bound by no territorial restrictions. Abbots Regular *de regimine*, provided they are priests and have legitimately received the abbatial blessing, are also conceded by the common law the faculty of conferring tonsure and minor orders. But they are exclusively restricted to candidates who are their subjects by reason of at least simple profession.[127]

Cardinals may ordain to tonsure and minor orders *any candidates*, anywhere in the world. But they are subject to one condition, the verification of which seems to be required for the *validity* of the ordination.[128] That condition is expressed in the words *"dummodo promovendus habeat dimissorias proprii Ordinarii litteras."* [129]

Dimissorial letters are required whenever a candidate is to be ordained by another than his own proper bishop.[130] For the *ordinary* minister, these letters are required only for the *licitness* of the ordination.[131] The *extraordinary* minister confers orders validly only when he observes all the norms and conditions to which his faculty is subject.[132] Therefore, the requirement of dimissorial letters affects the *validity* of an ordination conferred by a cardinal.

adnexa officio sive commissa personae, nequit aliis demandari, nisi id expresse fuerit iure vel indulto concessum. *Nota.* The power to confer Diaconate and Priesthood, which are certainly sacramental orders, is *potestas ordinis iuris divini*, and therefore cannot be delegated.

[126] Canon 957, § 2.

[127] Canon 964, n. 1.

[128] Cf. Sipos, *Enchiridion*, p. 453 (9), ad calcem.

[129] Canon 239, § 1, n. 22.

[130] Canon 955, § 1.

[131] Canon 962.

[132] Cappello, *De Sacra Ordinatione*, n. 263.

CHAPTER VI

PRIVILEGES THAT CONCERN THE CELEBRATION OF MASS

WITH regard to the celebration of the Holy Sacrifice of the Mass, numerous privileges have been granted to cardinals by the common law. These exemptions from the common law are enjoyed not only relative to the place for the celebration of Mass, but also regarding the times, i. e. days and hours, when Mass may be said.

ARTICLE I. THE ORATORIES OF CARDINALS

Canon 1189. Oratoria S.R.E. Cardinalium et Episcoporum sive residentialium sive titularium, licet privata, fruuntur tamen omnibus iuribus et privilegiis quibus oratoria semi-publica gaudent.

Canon 239, § 1, n. 18. Fruendi sacello ab Ordinario visitatione exempto.

Since many of the Masses said by a cardinal will be said in the oratory of his residence, mention must be made of the peculiar juridic status of such oratories. It is explicitly stated in the Code that the oratory of a cardinal's residence is juridically a private oratory which, however, by a privilege of the law enjoys all the rights and privileges of a semi-public oratory.[1]

The reason for devoting a special canon to this type of oratory is precisely this: had it not been expressly stated that such oratories are private oratories, they would not have been considered such. For the Code in declaring that private oratories are such as are erected in private houses,[2] would have been interpreted as thereby excluding the oratories of cardinals and bishops, since it was de-

[1] Canon 1189. Cf. canon 1188, § 2, nn. 2, 3.

[2] Canon 1188, § 2, n. 3.

clared by Pope Benedict XIV (1740-1758) that the houses of these dignitaries were not private houses.[3] In this letter Benedict XIV had reference to the decree of the Council of Trent prohibiting bishops from allowing either seculars or regulars to celebrate Mass in private houses.[4] Pope Benedict XIV expressly stated that this decree did not pertain to episcopal or cardinalitial residences as these were not private houses.

Such an interpretation had been implied earlier in a decree of the Sacred Congregation of the Council in which it was asserted that the oratories of cardinals were not comprehended in the decree of Paul V (1605-1621) prohibiting the celebration of Mass in private oratories without the permission of the Holy See.[5]

In view of these decrees the legislator of the Code desired to make it clear that the oratories of cardinals and bishops are private oratories, which, however, enjoy all the rights and privileges of semi-public oratories.

Feldhaus [6] asserts that these oratories constitute a distinct species of private oratories (1) since they are not erected in private houses, and (2) since they enjoy all the rights and privileges of semi-public oratories. They are to be termed private rather than domestic oratories.

Since these oratories enjoy all the rights and privileges of semi-public oratories, all sacred functions can be held therein except such as the rubrics or the orders of the bishop exclude.[7] Whereas in other domestic oratories only one Mass and that a low Mass can be

[3] Ep. encycl., *"Magno cum,"* 2 iun. 1751, 2—*Fontes,* n. 413.

[4] Conc. Trident., sess. XXII, c. 1, *De observandis et evitandis in celebratione Missae*—Schroeder, *Canons and Decrees of the Council of Trent,* p. 150.

[5] S.C.C., 18 feb. 1623: " . . . cappellas et Oratoria ad illorum (i. e., cardinales et episcopi) usum ubique locorum exstructa minime comprehendi in prohibitione Congregationis iussu san. mem. Paul V iam pridem edita (S.C.C., *Florentina,* 23 maii 1615—*Fontes,* n. 2396) de non celebrando in privatis oratoriis."—*Fontes,* n. 2436.

[6] *Oratories,* The Catholic University of America Canon Law Studies, n. 42 (Washington, D. C.: The Catholic University of America Press, 1927), p. 76.

[7] Cf. canon 1193.

read,[8] in the private oratories of cardinals (and bishops) many Masses can be said each day even when the cardinal is absent from his residence.[9]

Moreover, since a cardinal's oratory enjoys the rights and privileges of a semi-public oratory, any of the faithful attending Mass therein fulfill the obligation of a preceptive Mass.[10] This fact had been recognized by the Sacred Congregation of Rites as far back as the seventeenth century.[11] In 1896 a decree of the same congregation expressly mentioned the oratories of cardinals as enjoying this privilege.[12]

It may also be noted that the oratories of cardinals and bishops since they are similar by law to semi-public oratories may have a consecrated fixed altar, whereas the general law for domestic oratories does not permit a consecrated fixed altar.[13]

Finally, with reference to the oratories of cardinals, it must be remembered that cardinals enjoy no privilege from the common law allowing them to reserve the Blessed Sacrament in their oratories. Special permission of the Holy See is required in order to reserve the Blessed Sacrament therein. Should a cardinal have women re-

[8] Canon 1195, § 1.

[9] Cf. S.R.C., *Bituntina,* 2 iul. 1661—*Fontes,* n. 5529; *Bosanen,* 8 apr. 1854 —*Fontes,* n. 5970; Berutti, in *Jus Pontificium,* XIX (1939), p. 31.

[10] Canon 1249.

[11] S.R.C., *"Bituntina,"* 2 iul. 1661: ". . . In cappella Palatii Episcopalis, etiam absente Episcopo vel vacante sede, posse Missam celebrari potissimum vero per Vicarium; nec non diebus Festis inibi Sacrum audientes, implere preceptum Ecclesiae."—*Decreta Authentica Congregationis Sacrorum Rituum* (5 vols., Romae, Ex Typographia Polyglotta, 1898-1901), n. 1196. (Henceforth cited as *Decr. Auth.*); *Fontes,* n. 5529.

[12] S.R.C., *"Urbis et Orbis,"* 8 iun. 1896: "Postulandum a Sanctissimo, ut deinceps Episcopi omnes, sive Dioecesani, sive Titulares, eodem privilegio condecorentur, quo fruuntur Patres Cardinales, scilicet, ut, non solum ipsi in propriae habitationis Oratorio, aut super Ara portatili, ubicumque degant, Missam facere aliamque in sui commodum permittere valeant, sed etiam omnes fideles alterutram ex eisdem Missis audientes, quoties opus fuerit, praeceptum Ecclesiae adimpleant."—*Fontes,* n. 6261.

[13] Cf. Bliley, *Altars According to the Code of Canon Law,* The Catholic University of America Canon Law Studies, n. 38 (Washington, D. C.: The Catholic University of America, 1927), p. 77, hereafter cited *Altars.*

ligious taking care of his residence, then their presence would allow him to reserve the Blessed Sacrament without the need of special permission from the Holy See.

A second privilege is granted to cardinals' oratories, namely, that of being exempt from visitation by the local Ordinary.[14]

The general law concerning private oratories states that when the Holy See has granted an indult permitting Mass in a domestic or private oratory, then, unless the indult states otherwise one Mass can be *read* there daily excepting on the more solemn Feast days, but only after the local Ordinary has visited the oratory and found it to be well constructed and a fitting place for the celebration of Mass.[15] In private oratories not enjoying an Apostolic Indult, the Ordinary himself may grant permission *per modum actus* for Mass in an extraordinary case, but only after he has made a similar visitation.[16] From such visitations by the local Ordinary a cardinal's oratory is by privilege exempt. It is likewise exempt from the visitation that the bishop, at least quinquennially, must make of his diocese.[17]

Article II. Privilege of Celebrating Mass in Any Private Oratory Without Prejudice to the Owner's Indult Which Generally Allows Only One Mass Daily.

Canon 239, § 1, n. 14. Sacrum celebrandi in quolibet privato sacello sine praeiudicio illius qui indulto gaudet.

The general law contains the stipulation that unless the contrary is expressly stated in the indult, in domestic or private oratories that have been erected by indult of the Holy See, one Mass only can be read daily. On the more solemn Feasts of the Church not even this single Mass is permitted.[18] In view of this legislation

[14] Canon 239, § 1, n. 18.

[15] Canon 1195 together with canon 1192, § 2.

[16] Canon 1194 together with canon 1192, § 2; cf. Feldhaus, *Oratories*, pp. 119-129.

[17] Cf. canons 343 and 344, § 1.

[18] Canon 1195, § 1.

when one Mass has been read in such an oratory, no other priest may on the same day use the oratory for Mass.

Cardinals, however, in view of the privilege here being considered are not comprehended in this law. Thus, when a cardinal says Mass in such an oratory the indult of the owner remains intact and the usual daily Mass may still be read in the same domestic or private oratory.

This privilege seems to be new with the Code and is not shared with bishops.[19]

Article III. Privilege of Using a Portable Altar

Canon 239, § 1, n. 7. Celebrandi super aram portatilem non solum in domo propriae habitationis, sed ubicumque degunt, et permittendi ut alia Missa, ipsis adstantibus, celebretur.

Besides celebrating Mass in their own or another's private oratory, cardinals are privileged by law to make use of the portable altar, i. e., they enjoy the privilege of celebrating Mass upon a consecrated altar stone, in any place provided it be respectable and becoming.

This privilege has been enjoyed by cardinals for many centuries. Boniface VIII (1294-1303) originally granted it to bishops and *their superiors.*[20]

That cardinals were comprehended in the phrase *"eorumque superiores"* of that grant has been the constant teaching of canonists.[21]

[19] Cf. canon 349.

[20] C. 12, *de privilegiis,* V, 7, in VI°: "Quoniam episcopi eorumque superiores se habent diversis ex causis a suis ecclesiis et dioecesibus absentare frequenter, nec semper possunt commode ad ecclesias accedere pro missa celebranda vel audienda in ipsis, sine qua eos transire non decet absque causa rationabili ullam diem: praesenti constitutione indulgemus eisdem, ut altare possint habere viaticum, et in eo celebrare ac facere celebrari, ubicumque absque interdicti transgressione illis permittitur celebrare vel audire divina."

[21] Cf. Fagnanus, *Commentaria,* in c. 25, X, *de privilegiis et excessibus privilegiatorum,* V, 33, nn. 4-31; in c. 16, X, *de poenitentiis et remissionibus,* V, 38, n. 46; Diana, *Resolutiones Morales,* vol. 5, tom. 9, tract. 7, res. 49;

A decree of the Council of Trent [22] indirectly revoked all privileges hitherto granted to use the portable altar. It prescribed that the bishop should not permit the celebration of Mass in private houses or in places outside churches, or outside oratories dedicated to divine services. The observance of this decree bound both the secular and regular clergy. The decree *directly* mentioned only the places in which Mass should not be celebrated, but since Mass could only be celebrated in such places on a portable altar, it *indirectly* restricted the use of the portable altar.[23]

Though the decree seemed to comprehend the privilege of cardinals and bishops, their privileges were not abrogated. This is not apparent from the decree itself, but from subsequent decisions of the Sacred Congregation of Cardinals for the Interpretation of the Council of Trent.[24] In a decision of this Congregation dated February 18, 1623, it was made quite clear that cardinals still retained this privilege which they could use everywhere without the need of the local Ordinary's permission.[25]

The general law of the Code concerning the celebration of Mass stipulates that Mass must be said on a consecrated altar *and* in a church or oratory consecrated or blessed according to law.[26] To say Mass on a portable altar one must have a privilege conceded either by the common law or by Apostolic Indult.[27] Cardinals are granted such a privilege by the common law.[28] Consequently, they may cele-

Card. Petra, *Commentaria ad Constitutiones Apostolicas*, Vol. I, p. 87, n. 48; Plati, *De Dignitate et Officio Cardinalis*, Appendix I, nn. 62-70; Sägmüller, *Die Thätigkeit und Stellung der Cardinäle bis Papst Bonifaz VIII*, p. 150, II, c; Wernz, *Ius Decretalium*, II, n. 632.

[22] Sess. XXII, c. I, *De observandis et evitandis in celebratione Missae*—Schroeder, *Canons and Decrees of the Council of Trent*, p. 150.

[23] Cf. Bliley, *Altars*, p. 48.

[24] E.g., S.C.C., *Florentina*, 23 maii 1615—*Fontes*, n. 2396; cf. Gattico, *De Usu Altaris Portatilis* (Romae, 1746), cap. XII, nn. 1 sq.

[25] "Sacra etc. censuit S.R.E. Cardinales non secus atque episcopis sine ulla licentia Episcopi Dioecesani uti posse privilegio altaris portatilis ad praescriptum fel. rec. Bonifatii VIII, quae incipit 'Quoniam episcopi.' "—*Fontes*, n. 2436.

[26] Canon 822, § 1.

[27] Canon 822, § 2.

[28] Canon 239, § 1, n. 7. Bishops also enjoy this privilege by grant of com-

brate Mass upon a consecrated altar stone,[29] in any place that is respectable and becoming.[30] Canon 822, § 3 excludes from the privilege of a portable altar the celebration of Mass at sea. A priest, therefore, who has such a privilege is not thereby entitled to use it on a ship at sea without special indult from the Holy See.[31] Cardinals enjoy the added privilege of celebrating aboard ship while traveling at sea, not, however, in virtue of the privilege of the portable altar, but, as will be seen, in virtue of a separate and distinct privilege which will be treated in the subsequent article of this chapter.

This portable altar privilege allows cardinals to celebrate Mass not only in an unconsecrated or unblessed place, but also in a place not destined for divine worship. This extends even to a bedroom, for, as Bliley argues,[32] the clause forbidding the celebration of Mass upon a portable altar in a bedroom, mentioned in canon 822, § 3, has reference to the permission granted *per modum actus* by the bishop or other Ordinary of the place to celebrate Mass on a portable altar outside a church or oratory. If the Holy See therefore, grants the privilege either in the common law or by indult without expressly forbidding its use in a bedroom, a bedroom in itself is not excluded. Should the bedroom be very small or unbecoming for some other reason, it would be excluded by force of the general law as a place not becoming for the celebration of Mass.[33]

Joined to the cardinal's personal faculty of celebrating Mass on a portable altar is the faculty of permitting another Mass to be celebrated in his presence. Thus, while the cardinal is making his

mon law (canon 349). Simple priests may also enjoy this privilege. When they do, they enjoy it through Apostolic Indult not by grant of the common law. Moreover, such an indult ordinarily permits the celebration of Mass by the priest-grantee alone. Consequently, he cannot, like a cardinal or bishop, allow another priest to say Mass on the portable altar in his presence. For a complete list of those who by common law enjoy the grant of the portable altar, cf. Bliley, *Altars*, p. 112 sq.

[29] Cf. canon 1197, § 1, n. 2.

[30] Canon 822, § 3.

[31] Apostolic Nuncios and Delegates can grant this indult by virtue of n. 37 of their faculties. Cf. Bouscaren, *Digest*, I, 182.

[32] *Altars*, p. 111.

[33] Cf. Coronata, *De Locis et Temporibus Sacris* (Augustae Taurinorum: Marietti, 1922), n. 127, p. 127.

thanksgiving he can permit another priest to offer Mass on the portable altar. Contained in the same section of canon 239, this is an added privilege, for the privilege of the portable altar when granted by indult is strictly for the benefit of the one to whom it is granted and cannot be extended to another priest. This extension of the cardinalitial privilege was contained in the original grant of Boniface VIII,[34] and is clearly granted for the convenience of the cardinals so that, e. g. when sick and not able to say Mass themselves, they may have a priest celebrate on a portable altar in their bedroom. For the privilege to be extended to another priest it is not necessary that the cardinal also celebrate, but it is necessary that the other priest say the Mass in the cardinal's presence.[35] The cardinal's presence is required because the privilege is a personal one having reference to the person of the cardinal.

Finally, any of the faithful who hear Mass said on a portable altar either by the cardinal himself or by another priest to whom the cardinal has extended the privilege, fulfill the obligation of a preceptive Mass. This was declared by the Sacred Congregation of Rites in a decree dated June 8, 1896,[36] and as Bliley,[37] following Coronata,[38] states, this decree does not seem to have been revoked.

Article IV. Privilege of Celebrating Mass at Sea

Canon 239, § 1, n. 8. Celebrandi in mari, debitis cautelis adhibitis.

The faculty of celebrating Mass aboard ship while traveling at sea must always come from the Holy See. This was expressed by Benedict XIV (1740-1758).[39]

[34] ". . . indulgemus eisdem, ut altare possint habere viaticum, et in eo celebrare *ac facere celebrari*. . . ." Italics are the writer's.

[35] Cf. Coronata, *op. cit.*, n. 124, pp. 126-127.

[36] *Fontes*, n. 6261. This decree which referred both to Mass said in a cardinal's oratory or on a portable altar is quoted above, p. ??, footnote, n. ?.

[37] *Altars*, p. 113.

[38] *Op. cit.*, n. 124, p. 126.

[39] Const. "*Aestas*," 11 oct. 1757, n. XXIII—*Fontes*, n. 445.

In virtue of his faculties the Apostolic Delegate may grant permission to celebrate Mass aboard ship on a portable altar.[40]

A decree of the Sacred Congregation of Rites declared that permission to celebrate Mass at sea could not be granted by the proper Ordinary of the priest, nor by the bishop of the diocese from which the ship sails.[41]

As has been noted the privilege of a portable altar expressly prohibits its use at sea.[42] Therefore, even if a priest enjoys the privilege of a portable altar, he needs a special indult to use it aboard a ship.[43] Such an indult is necessary even if the ship has its own semi-public oratory as did the Italian liners *Rex* and *Conte di Savoia.*[44]

Cardinals, however, by virtue of the common law[45] enjoy this special faculty of celebrating Mass on a ship at sea and this privilege is new with the Code. Cardinals may, therefore, celebrate Mass whenever they travel at sea on board a ship, *provided they observe* the necessary precautions (*"debitis cautelis adhibitis"*). These precautions are (1) that the sea be calm and there be no danger of irreverence, e. g. of spilling the Precious Blood; (2) that another priest assist, e. g. to keep the chalice secure should the sea become rough after the Mass has been started.[46]

The Mass may be said in a private cabin unless the cabin is so

[40] Cf. Faculties (Private), C. IV, n. 37: "To permit priests who are journeying either by sea or over streams, to celebrate Mass on board ship on a portable altar, provided there be nothing unbecoming about the place where the Mass is celebrated, and there be no danger of the spilling of the Precious Blood."—Bouscaren, *Digest,* I, p. 182.

[41] S.R.C. *Vicen.,* 4 mar. 1901—*ASS,* XXXIII (1900-1901), 679.

[42] Canon 822, § 3: Hoc privilegium ita intelligendum est, ut secumferat facultatem ubique celebrandi, honesto tamen ac decenti loco et super petram sacram, *non autem in mari.* (Italics are the writer's.)

[43] Cf. Cappello, *De Sacramentis,* Vol. I (Romae, 1928), n. 753.

[44] Cf. Coronata, *De Locis et Temporibus Sacris,* n. 77, p. 78, nota (1) ad calcem.

[45] Canon 239, § 1, n. 8. Bishops also share this privilege (canon 349).

[46] Cf. Ben. XIV, *Aestas,* 11 oct. 1757, n. xxiii—*Fontes,* n. 445; S.C. de Prop. Fid., 1 martii, 1902—*Collectanea,* n. 2130; Cappello, *De Sacramentis,* Vol. I, n. 753; Coronata, *op. cit.,* n. 77, p. 78, nota (1) ad calcem.

small that it would not be considered a becoming place for the celebration of Mass.[47]

The privilege is not strictly limited to *ocean* voyages, but may be used when traveling aboard ship on a lake or river, e. g. while taking a cruise on the Great Lakes. This follows from the fact that the term *"ocean voyage"* has been interpreted to include lakes and rivers.[48]

One might argue that the faculty to say Mass on a lake or river boat is included in the privilege of a portable altar since the Code prohibits its use only on the ocean or at sea (*"in mari"*).[49] Such an interpretation, however, cannot be sustained in view of the following facts. (1) As has been noted above, the term *"ocean voyage"* has been interpreted to include lakes and rivers. Consequently, if a portable altar cannot be used at sea or on the ocean without a special indult, it likewise cannot be used on a lake or river boat without a special indult. (2) The wording of the Apostolic Delegate's faculty in this regard is to grant the faculty to say Mass on shipboard "to priests who are journeying either by sea *or over streams. . . .*"[50]

In view of these facts, the faculty of saying Mass on a lake or river boat is not comprehended in the privilege of the portable altar, but requires a separate and distinct indult which cardinals are granted by the common law.

Article V. Privilege of Enjoying on Any Day the Benefit of the Personally Privileged Altar

Canon 239, § 1, n. 10. Fruendi altari privilegiato personali quotidiano.

In celebrating Mass, Cardinals are further privileged by law in as much as they daily enjoy a personal privileged altar. This privilege which is new with the Code is also enjoyed by Bishops.[51]

[47] S.C. de Prop. Fid., 13 aug. 1902—*ASS,* XXV (1902-1903), 612; Coronata, *loc. cit.*

[48] S.C. de Prop. Fid., 27 iun. 1914—Sylloge, n. 51; cf. Bouscaren, *Digest,* II (1943), p. 219.

[49] Canon 833, § 3.

[50] Italics are the writer's. Cf. Bouscaren, *Digest,* I, 182.

[51] Cf. canon 349.

An altar is said to be privileged when, in addition to the ordinary fruits of the Eucharistic Sacrifice, a plenary indulgence is also granted *per modum suffragii* whenever Mass is offered thereon for the soul of one of the faithful departed. Wherefore, the privilege of this kind of an altar consists in a plenary indulgence, which, as far as the intention of the Holy Father and the use of the power of the keys extend, is sufficient in itself to free forthwith a soul from the pains of purgatory; but as far as the efficacy of application is concerned, it must be left to the divine mercy and acceptance.[52] Hence, this indulgence, like every indulgence applied to the souls in purgatory, is applied "*per modum suffragii*";[53] for, although the Roman Pontiff offers to God from the treasury of the Church a price sufficient to liberate a soul immediately from the pains of purgatory, God is not bound to accept this price. Hence, the acceptance or the measure of the acceptance depends on the mercy of God.[54]

The faculty of the privileged altar is of two kinds: (1) *Local or real,* when the privilege is annexed to the altar itself so that every priest who celebrates Mass at such an altar enjoys the privilege. (2) *Personal,* when the privilege is granted to a priest, so that it does not depend upon a certain altar, but on the priest who celebrates. Hence, on whatever altar he celebrates, whether it be fixed or portable, the altar he uses is for the time being a privileged altar.[55]

The cardinals' privilege as canon 239 indicates is personal. Consequently, whenever a cardinal offers Mass for the soul of one of the faithful departed, whether on a fixed or portable altar, in addition to the ordinary fruits of the Sacrifice, a plenary indulgence is granted *per modum suffragii.*

The indulgence may be applied only to the deceased person for whom the cardinal is offering Mass. If a cardinal is offering Mass for a living person, then the indulgence cannot be applied, for although an altar is sometimes privileged by way of special indult

[52] S.C. Indulg., 28 iul. 1840—*Decreta Authentica Sacrae Congregationis Indulgentiis Sacrisque Reliquis Praepositae* (Ratisbone, 1883), n. 283. (Hereafter cited as *Decr. Auth. S.C. Ind.*).

[53] Cf. canon 911.

[54] Cf. Cappello, *De Sacramentis,* I, n. 760.

[55] Cf. Bliley, *Altars,* p. 123.

pro vivis et defunctis, though such cases are rare, this seems to be true only of *local* privileges and even then it must be clearly expressed in the indult.[56]

The Mass and the indulgence are not to be separated by the cardinal but must be applied together for the same deceased person.[57] Indults sometimes permit the offering of the Mass for one deceased person and the application of the indulgence to another.[58] The cardinals' privilege, however, is to be understood in the usual acceptation of the privilege *of the altar,* namely, that the plenary indulgence must be applied to the deceased person for whose soul the Mass is being offered.

If a cardinal is offering Mass for many deceased persons, the indulgence cannot be applied to all of them but must be limited to one of them previously determined by the cardinal-celebrant.[59] If he is offering Mass both for the living and the deceased, then, since he cannot separate the application of the indulgence from the application of the Mass, the indulgence of the privileged altar cannot be applied to the soul of one of the deceased persons.[60]

To apply the indulgence, however, it is not necessary to make a separate intention. Consequently, whenever a cardinal says Mass for the soul of one deceased person, the plenary indulgence attached to his privilege is *ipso facto* applied to that soul.[61]

That the indulgence of the privileged altar be gained, it is not necessary that the celebrant of the Mass be in the state of grace. Cappello holds this opinion to be certain since the efficacy of the

[56] Cf. Blat, *Commentarium,* Lib. III, Pars I (Romae, 1924), n. 250, p. 305.

[57] S.C. Indulg., 5 aug. 1897—*ASS,* XXX (1897-1898), 278.

[58] Such was the general indult enjoyed by all priests during the Jubilee Year of 1929, cf. Bull of Pius XI—*AAS,* XXI (1929), 5, 168; Bouscaren, *Digest* I, 433-434. The same interpretation was given to the general indult granted by Pius XII to be valid from May 13, 1942, to May 13, 1943. Cf. *AAS,* XXXIV (1942), 153, 210; Bouscaren, *Digest,* II, 223-224.

[59] S.C. Indulg., 29 feb. 1864, ad I, 19 iun. 1880, ad 2—*Decr. Auth. S. C. Ind.,* nn. 402, 451; S. Poenit. (Sect. de Indulg.), 6 iul. 1917, ad I—*AAS,* IX (1917), 440.

[60] Bliley, *Altars,* p. 125; Cappello, *De Sacramentis,* I, n. 761.

[61] S.C. Indulg., 12 martii 1855—*Decr. Auth. S. C. Ind.,* n. 366; S. Off. (Sect. de Indulg.), 17 iun. 1915—*AAS,* VII (1915), 410.

privilege is not based on the personal dispositions of the priest but flows entirely *"ex suffragio ecclesiae."* [62]

Finally, under the present legislation of the Church, one is not obliged to say the *Missa de Requie* or to add the special prayer of the dead in the ferial Mass or Mass of a vigil, as was formerly required; nevertheless, the Holy See has stated it to be fitting and proper that the votive Mass for the dead, or the ferial Mass or Mass of a vigil with the prayer for the deceased person, be said when the rubrics of the Missal permit.[63]

Article VI. Privilege of Offering a Private Mass on Holy Thursday and of Celebrating Successively From Midnight Three Private Masses on Christmas

Canon 239, § 1, n. 4. Celebrandi vel alii permittendi ut coram se celebret unam Missam in Feria V maioris hebdomadae ac tres Missas in nocte Nativitatis Domini.

Another favorable exception to the general law is enjoyed by cardinals relative to the celebration of Mass. Definite legislation has been enacted to govern the times at which Mass may be celebrated. Canon 820 states that Mass may be celebrated every day of the year except on those days excluded by the priest's proper rite. In the Roman rite private Masses are forbidden on Holy Thursday. This prohibition is gathered from two decrees of the Sacred Congregation of Rites.[64]

The cardinalitial privilege here being considered is an exemption from the general prohibition and permits cardinals to celebrate a private Mass or have a priest celebrate such a Mass in their presence on Holy Thursday.[65] A similar exemption is had with regard to

[62] *De Sacramentis,* I, n. 764.

[63] S.C.S. Off. (Sect. de Indulg.), 20 feb. 1913—*AAS,* V (1913), 122.

[64] *Urbis,* 28 mar. 1775, ad V—*Decr. Auth.*, n. 2503; *Resolutionis dubiorum,* 28 iul. 1821—*Decr. Auth.,* n. 2616. Cf. Rubric at the end of the Mass for Wednesday of Holy Week; Gasparri, *De Sanctissima Eucharistia* (2 vols., Parisiis et Lugduni, 1897), I, nn. 74-75; Cappello, *De Sacramentis,* I, n. 784; canon 862.

[65] Bishops also enjoy this privilege. Cf. canon 349.

saying three private Masses successively from midnight on Christmas. The stipulation of the general law is that Mass shall not be begun earlier than one hour before dawn, except on Christmas Day, when it is permitted in parochial and conventual churches to say *one* Mass at midnight. To follow this immediately with one or both the other Masses permitted by the liturgy of the day requires an apostolic indult. Also on Christmas Day religious houses or charitable institutions having an oratory with the faculty of reserving the Blessed Sacrament are permitted to have one priest celebrate successively from midnight the three Masses permitted by the liturgy of the day.[66]

The cardinalitial privilege exempts cardinals from this legislation and permits them to celebrate successively from midnight and privately the three Masses of Christmas Day.[67] If the cardinal does not make use of the privilege himself, the canon permits him to allow another priest to celebrate these Christmas Masses in his presence.

The episcopal privilege in this regard is qualified by the phrase, *"dummodo non teneantur celebrare in cathedrali."* Residential bishops are generally obliged to celebrate Mass solemnly in the cathedral on Holy Thursday.[68] Therefore, a cardinal who is also a residential bishop cannot personally say another private Mass on Holy Thursday, but he may permit another priest to celebrate such a Mass in his presence.[69]

In virtue of this privilege either the cardinal *or* another priest at the cardinal's behest may celebrate at such times. It is not permitted that both celebrate.[70] From the use of the disjunctive *"vel"* instead of *aut*, it might be argued that the legislator meant to permit both a cardinal *and* another priest to celebrate such Masses, since in strict classical latinity the disjunctive *vel* has the meaning of one or the other *or both*, whereas *aut* signifies one or the other, *not both*. In the Code, however, one cannot argue from the proper meaning of conjunctions and disjunctives, for as Morsdorf points out in his

[66] Canon 821.

[67] Canon 239, § 1, n. 4. Bishops have a similar privilege (canon 349).

[68] Cf. canon 734, § 1.

[69] Coronata, *Institutiones*, I, n. 401, (i).

[70] Cf. Blat, *Commentarium*, Lib. II, n. 205.

recent work on the use of latin terminology in the Code [71] such words are used interchangeably in the Code so that they do not always have their strict classical meaning or connotation. To the writer, in view of the following arguments, "*vel*" seems to have been used here in the strict classical sense of *aut,* the signification being that such Masses may be said by one or the other, *not by both.* Blat holds this interpretation to be certain.[72] It seems more correct, firstly from the fact that this is a privilege granted for the personal benefit of a cardinal so that as a recognition of his dignity in the universal Church he may say a private Mass e. g., on Holy Thursday when the general law forbids such Masses, or, if he is unable to celebrate personally, for instance, because of ill health, he may permit such a Mass to be said in his presence. Secondly, that this is the proper interpretation seems to follow from the fact that in this same canon in the section that treats of the portable altar privilege, the legislator in indicating that two Masses may be said does so in clear and unequivocal language.[73] In view of these points, the privilege is to be interpreted as meaning that on Holy Thursday either the cardinal or another priest, *not both,* may celebrate a private Mass, and that on Christmas Day either the cardinal or another priest, *not both,* may celebrate three Masses successively from midnight.

Article VII. Privilege of Using Own Ordo and Assistant Priest

Canon 239, § 1, n. 9. In omnibus ecclesiis et oratoriis Missam celebrandi proprio calendario conformem.

Canon 812. Nulli sacerdoti celebranti, praeter Episcopos aliosque praelatos usu pontificalium fruentes, licet, sola honoris aut solemnitatis causa, habere presbyterem assistentem.

[71] Görres-Gesellschaft, Vol. 74: *Die Rechtssprache des Codex Juris Canonici* (Paderborn: Verlag Ferdinand Schöningh, 1937), p. 31, vii.

[72] *Loc. cit.*

[73] Canon 239, § 1, n. 7: ". . . *et* permittendi ut *alia* Missa, ipsis adstantibus, celebretur." (Italics are the writer's.)

Section 1. Using Own Ordo

With regard to the type of Mass to be said by a priest, each diocese has its own special calendar, set forth in the local *Ordo,* made up of the calendar of the universal Church (as found in the beginning of the Roman Missal and the Róman Breviary) with the addition of the local feasts of the Dedication of the Cathedral, the Titular of the Cathedral, the Dedication of all churches of the diocese (which have been consecrated), the feasts of the principal and secondary patrons of the diocese and of the nation and province to which the diocese belongs, and the feast of local saints (the celebration of which has been granted by the Holy See). Regular Orders together with the communities of nuns and sisters of these Orders, Congregations and Institutes of both sexes which are approved by the Holy See and are constituted under one general superior and are bound to the recitation of the Divine Office—all these have an entirely proper *Ordo.*[74]

Accordingly, the *Ordo* to be followed for the celebration of Mass is, in general, the diocesan *Ordo;* in the churches and oratories of Religious who have a proper *Ordo,* their proper *Ordo;* in the churches and oratories of Religious who have not a proper calendar, the diocesan *Ordo.*

The general law relative to the *Ordo* to be followed by a priest celebrating Mass in a church to which he is not attached, is based on three decrees of the Sacred Congregation of Rites. These decrees state that each and every priest, whether secular or regular, is to say Mass, even a Mass that is proper to Regulars, according to the Calendar (*Ordo*) of the church or public oratory in which he celebrates, excluding, however, special rites of Orders,[75] or churches.[76]

[74] Cf. O'Connell, *The Celebration of Mass* (3 vols., Milwaukee: Bruce Publishing Co., 1940-1941), I, p. 57. Congregations or Institutes, whether approved by the Holy See or by the Ordinary of the diocese only, if they are not constituted under one general superior, have not a proper *Ordo,* but follow the *Ordo* of the diocese, with the addition of certain special Offices that have been granted by the Holy See.

[75] E. g., the Dominican or Cistercian Rite.

[76] E. g., the rite of Bayeux of Lyon.

The same rule is to be observed in the semi-public oratory or principal chapel of seminaries, colleges, pious communities, hospitals, prisons and the like. If votive or other Masses are permitted by the calendar of the church or oratory, they may be celebrated, observing the rubrics and decrees.[77] In a semi-public oratory that is not the principal chapel of such a house, and in private oratories, the priest is to follow his own proper *Ordo*.[78]

Cardinals, however, when celebrating outside their proper churches are exempted from these regulations in virtue of a privilege newly granted them by the Code.[79]

In whatever church or oratory (public, semi-public or private) cardinals celebrate Mass, they may use the *Ordo* that is proper to each of them. That means that if a cardinal is actively attached to the Curia in Rome, he may use the proper *Ordo* of the diocese of Rome wherever he celebrates Mass. If the cardinal is a residential bishop outside of Rome, he may always follow the *Ordo* of his diocese, whether saying Mass in a Religious house within the diocese or celebrating in churches and oratories outside that diocese. Should the cardinal be a member of a Religious group that has its proper *Ordo*, then he may use that *Ordo* in any church or oratory throughout the world in which he celebrates Mass.

Section 2. Using an Assistant Priest

In Canon 812 which is quoted at the beginning of this article, it is stated that no one except bishops and other prelates who enjoy the use of the pontificals may have an assistant priest when celebrating Mass. That cardinals are comprehended in the phrase *"aliosque praelatos usu pontificalium fruentes"* is clear from nn. 13 and 15 of Canon 239.[80]

[77] S.R.C., *Urbis et Orbis,* 9 iul.-9 dec., 1895—*Decr. Auth.*, n. 3862; *Ruthenen.*, 22 maii 1896—*Decr. Auth.*, n. 3910. These decrees are quoted in the Rubrics of the Missal, *Additiones,* IV, 6.

[78] S.R.C., *Canonicorum Regularium Lateranensium Congregationis Austriacae,* 11 febr. 1910—*Decr. Auth.*, n. 4248; also, S.R.C., 14 maii 1926—*AAS,* XVIII (1926), 320.

[79] Canon 239, § 1, n. 9. Bishops also share this privilege with cardinals.

[80] Cf. *above*, pp. 25, 28.

Therefore, in a pontifical Mass a cardinal may use an assistant priest vested in a cope.[81] In virtue of this privilege a cardinal, like a bishop, may also use a priest vested only in cassock and surplice assisting at the missal even in a private Mass.[82]

Two other privileges that a cardinal enjoys in the celebration of Mass, namely the use of the zucchetto or skull-cap and the use of the ring, have already been treated in the chapter on the cardinals' privilege of dress.[83]

[81] Cf. *Caeremoniale Episcoporum*, I, Cap. VII.

[82] Cf. *Caeremoniale Episcoporum*, I, Cap. XXIX.

[83] Cf. *above* p. 22ff.

CHAPTER VII

PRIVILEGES THAT CONCERN VARIOUS SACRAMENTALS

Canon 239, § 1, n. 5. Benedicendi ubique, solo crucis signo, cum omnibus indulgentiis a Sancta Sede concedi solitis, rosaria, aliasque coronas precatorias, curces, numismata, statuas, scapularia a Sede Apostolica probata eaque imponendi sine onere inscriptionis;

Canon 239, § 1, n. 6. Sub unica benedictione erigendi, in ecclesiis et oratoriis etiam privatis aliisque piis locis, stationes *Viae Crucis* cum omnibus indulgentiis, quae huiusmodi pium exercitium peragentibus impertitae sunt; nec non benedicendi pro fidelibus, qui causa infirmatatis vel alius legitimi impedimenti sacras stationes *Viae Crucis* visitare nequeant, Crucifixi icones cum applicatione omnium indulgentiarum devoto exercitio eiusdem *Viae Crucis* a Romanis Pontificibus adnexarum;

Canon 239, § 1, n. 12. Benedicendi ubique populo more Episcoporum; sed in Urbe in ecclesiis tantum, piis locis et fiedelium consessibus;

Canon 239, § 1, n. 20. Consecrationes et benedictiones ecclesiarum, altarium, sacrae supellectilis, Abbatum aliasve similes, excepta oleorum sacrorum consecratione, si Cardinalis charactere episcopali careat, ubique locorum, servatis servandis, peragendi, firmo praescripto canon 1157.

Similarly to the many privileges enjoyed by cardinals relative to the administration of the Sacraments we find the common law conceding them numerous privileges apropos of the sacramentals.

The Code defines sacramentals as sacred objects or actions which the Church, in a certain imitation of the sacraments, employs for the purpose of obtaining favors, especially spiritual ones, through her intercession.[1] Clerics alone are the legitimate ministers of the sacramentals, for the administration of a sacramental is a ministerial act exercised in the name of the Church, hence it requires the power of orders which only clerics can obtain. The power of orders required in the cleric will depend upon the nature of the sacramental to be administered.[2]

Some of the sacred actions instituted by the Church as sacramentals fall under the general heading of *benedictiones.* These are variously divided.[3] By reason of their minister they are *reserved* or *unreserved* benedictions; by reason of their subject they are divided into *personal, real* or *local;* by reason of the rite used in performing them they are *solemn* or *private;* by reason of the form used they are *real* or *verbal;* by reason of their effect they are divided into *constitutive* benedictions, i. e. those that permanently consecrate or dedicate their subject—person, place or thing—to God, and *invocative* benedictions, i. e. those that call down the *benignitas Dei* upon the subject. Finally, benedictions are divided into *consecrations* and *blessings properly so called.*

Consecrations and blessings properly so-called are similar inasmuch as they withdraw things from profane usage and ascribe them to sacred usage. They differ, however, in many ways. A *Consecration* is a solemn blessing that always implies the use of the sacred oils. It is always a constitutive blessing. A *Benediction* (or blessing properly so called) is a private or simple blessing in which not the sacred oils, but holy water is used with accompanying prayers and signs. It can be either constitutive or invocative.[4] With regard to the administration of both of these cardinals have been granted many privileges.

[1] Canon 1144.

[2] Canon 1146: Paschang, *The Sacramentals according to the Code of Canon Law,* The Catholic University of America Canon Law Studies, n. 28 (Washington, D. C.: The Catholic University of America, 1925), pp. 36-38, hereafter cited *Sacramentals.*

[3] Cf. Paschang, *op. cit.*, pp. 48, 49.

[4] Cf. Beste, *Introductio in Codicem,* p. 553.

Article I. Consecrations of Churches, Altars, Chalices and Patens

Consecrations are by law reserved to bishops so that no one who lacks the episcopal character can validly perform consecrations unless he is permited to do so either by the common law or by apostolic indult.[5] Cardinals, even though not bishops, are granted this faculty by the common law,[6] which permits them to consecrate churches, altars and sacred furnishings, i. e., chalices and patens. If lacking the episcopal character, however, they are not permitted to bless the oils necessary for such acts, but must use the oils blessed by a bishop. In virtue of this faculty they may *validly* perform these consecrations *everywhere* even without the consent of the local Ordinary. This consent which is ordinarily required[7] affects only the licitness of a consecration performed by a cardinal, for *a iure* they have the necessary power mentioned in canon 1147. The power of cardinals in relation to consecrations is *potestas ordinis sed iuris mere ecclesiastici*,[8] which in accordance with canon 210 cannot be delegated since no express permission to do so is included in the grant.

Relative to the consecration of churches and altars, the various requisites of the law must of course be observed.[9] Canon 1157 rules

[5] Canon 1147, § 1.

[6] Canon 239, § 1, n. 20 as quoted at beginning of chapter.

[7] Cf. canon 1157.

[8] Cf. Cappello, *De Sacramentis*, Vol. II, Pars. III: *De Sacra Ordinatione* (Romae: Marietti, 1935), n. 289.

[9] Regarding the necessity and the requirements for consecrating churches and altars, many stipulations are made by the common law. Firstly, for Mass to be celebrated on an altar, whether fixed or portable, it must be consecrated (canon 822, § 1). Divine worship cannot take place in a new church until it has been dedicated (canon 1165, § 1). *Dedication* is a sacred rite instituted by the Church in virtue of which a profane place is rendered sacred and is perpetually destined to divine worship by a lawful minister. If the rite of dedication is solemnly administered it is called *consecration*; otherwise it is known as simple dedication or *blessing*. The Code requires that cathedral churches be dedicated by consecration and recommends dedication by consecration whenever possible for collegiate, conventual and parochial churches. It requires all churches to be dedicated at least by blessing (canon 1165, § 1). Public Oratories must be dedicated at least by blessing before sacred functions can be performed there-

that the consent of the local Ordinary is always required for the blessing or consecration of a sacred place. In consecrating a church or altar of their title cardinals do not have to comply with the regulation of canon 1157, that is, seek the consent of the Cardinal Vicar of the city, for canon 1155, § 1, expressly contains such a privilege.[10] Consequently, only when a cardinal consecrates a church or altar that does not pertain to his title must he obtain the consent of the local Ordinary, and that only for the licitness of the act.[11]

As Ziolkowski [12] points out, both Coronata and Augustine erroneously imply that a cardinal who is not a bishop cannot consecrate a church other than the church of his title. Augustine [13] writes: "Cardinals who are endowed with the episcopal character may, in virtue of a special privilege, consecrate churches and altars everywhere with the consent of the local ordinary." Coronata [14] asserts: "Minister validae et licitae consecrationis est: "Cardinales S.R.E. licet non episcopi pro ecclesiis et altaribus sui tituli; etiam extra proprios titulos de licentia tamen Ordinarii, si episcopali charactere insigniti sint." In pointing out these erroneous implications Ziolkowski [15] rightfully states that while it is true that the act of conse-

in; they may also be dedicated by consecration (canon 1191, § 2). Domestic oratories may neither be consecrated nor blessed after the manner of churches (canon 1196, § 1). With reference to semi-public oratories the Code contains neither an obligation nor a prohibition relative to dedicating them. But, both domestic and semi-public oratories if not dedicated, may be blessed with the ordinary "Benedictio loci vel domus" contained in the Ritual. Chalices and patens to be used in the Holy Sacrifice of the Mass must be consecrated. For a complete treatment of these points cf. Ziolkowski, *Consecration and Blessing of Churches,* The Catholic University of America Canon Law Studies, n. 187 (Washington, D. C.: The Catholic University of America Press, 1943), pp. 36-77; Feldhaus, *Oratories,* pp. 84-89, 115; Bliley, *Altars,* pp. 75-88, 103-107.

[10] Canon 1155, § 1: Consecratio alicuius loci spectat ad Ordinarium territorii in quo locus ipse reperitur . . . firmo iure S.R.E. Cardinalium consecrandi ecclesiam et altaria sui tituli.

[11] Cf. Ziolkowski, *The Consecration and Blessing of Churches,* p. 89.

[12] *The Consecration and Blessing of Churches,* p. 89.

[13] *A Commentary on the New Code of Canon Law* (8 vols., St. Louis: Herder, Vol. IV, 3. ed., *Administrative Law,* 1931), VI, 4, hereafter cited *Commentary.*

[14] *De Locis et Temporibus Sacris,* n. 5.

[15] *Loc. cit.*

cration is proper to the power of the episcopal order, nevertheless, the power to consecrate a church or altar derives merely from ecclesiastical law. The general law or the Roman Pontiff can grant to persons who are not endowed with the episcopal character the faculty of consecrating places and things. The law which grants to all cardinals, even those who lack the episcopal character, the power to consecrate churches and altars does prohibit them from blessing the holy oils if they lack the episcopal character, but it does not prohibit cardinals from consecrating churches and altars everywhere if they lack the episcopal character.[16]

The use of the words *"servatis servandis"* indicates that a cardinal using this privilege of consecrating is to observe the rite contained in the *Pontificale Romanum.*

In virtue of canon 1166, § 3, a cardinal who consecrates a church or altar in any place may concede on that day an indulgence of 300 days.[17] This indulgence may be conceded by the cardinal even though he has no jurisdiction over the territory and it may be gained by all those who visit the church on the day of its consecration.

The canon uses the words *"episcopus consecrator,"* but, as Ziolkowski notes, this term has reference to a minister who consecrates a church or altar in virtue of ordinary power.[18] Consequently, all cardinals, even those not endowed with the episcopal character, may grant such an indulgence on the occasion of consecrating a church or altar, for their power to consecrate such objects must be considered ordinary power since it is annexed to their office *ipso iure.*

Article II. Blessings

It is stated in the Code that blessings (benedictions in the strict sense of the term) may be administered by any priest except the

[16] Cf. canon 239, § 1, n. 20 as quoted at beginning of chapter.

[17] Canon 1166, § 3 mentions for cardinals an indulgence of 200 days. This has been recently augmented by a decree of Pope Pius XII who, on the occasion of his twenty-fifth anniversary as a bishop, decreed that in the future cardinals may grant an indulgence of 300 days instead of the 200 days mentioned in the Code. *AAS,* XXXIV (1942), 240; *The Jurist,* III (1943), 157-158.

[18] *Op. cit.,* p. 125.

blessings that are reserved to the Roman Pontiff, to bishops or to others.[19]

Blessings reserved to the Holy See include the blessing of the Pallium, the blessing of the Golden Rose, the blessing of the *Agnus Dei* and the blessing of the Royal Sword.[20] Various blessings are reserved to Ordinaries by the Code, e. g., the simple dedication of churches,[21] the simple blessing of cemeteries,[22] the blessing of Abbots and Prelates *nullius* [23] and the blessing of Regular Abbots *de regimine*.[24] The Roman Ritual contains many other blessings reserved to Ordinaries or their delegates.[25]

Other blessings such as those of the rosary and other prayer beads, scapulars and the Stations of the Cross are reserved to various Religious Orders by the Holy See. These also may be found in the Appendix of the Roman Ritual.

Cardinalitial privileges relative to reserved blessings are many and varied.

Section 1. Faculties in Which the Prescribed Form Is to Be Used

A. *Churches.* Cardinals are privileged to administer the blessing by which a church that is not being consecrated is dedicated.[26] The general law reserves this *benedictio* to the local Ordinary, or, in the case of clerical exempt religious, to the major superior.[27] In so dedicating a church by blessing, cardinals are to obtain the consent of the proper Ordinary for the licitness of the act.[28]

B. *Oratories.* Since public oratories are comprehended in the laws that govern churches,[29] the cardinalitial privilege of blessing

[19] Canon 1147, § 2.

[20] Cf. Paschang, *Sacramentals*, p. 57.

[21] Canon 1156.

[22] Canon 1205.

[23] Canon 322, § 2.

[24] Canon 625.

[25] Cf. *Rituale Romanum* (Ed. iuxta typicam Vaticanam, Mechliniae: H. Dessain, 1929), Appendix.

[26] Canon 239, § 1, n. 20 as quoted at beginning of chapter.

[27] Canon 1156.

[28] Canon 1157; Ziolkowski, *op. cit.*, p. 93.

[29] Cf. canon 1191, § 1.

churches extends also to the blessing of public oratories. Again, for the licitness of the act the consent of the proper Ordinary is required.

C. *Sacra Suppellex.* Comprehended also within the cardinalitial privilege of performing certain reserved blessings is the faculty of blessing the sacred furnishings (*sacra suppellex*) used at the altar. Under this heading of sacred furnishings are included ciboria, pyxes, ostensoria, oil stocks, sacred vestments and other furnishings or fixtures in the various phases of divine worship.[80] In blessing those sacred furnishings that require a blessing, cardinals are to use the various formulas given in the Roman Ritual for the individual objects.

D. *Abbatial Blessings.* Certain Abbots and Prelates *nullius* are at times required either by Apostolic precept or by the proper constitutions of their Order to receive the abbatial blessing. In fulfilling this requirement they are permitted to select any bishop to administer this blessing.[81] Regular Abbots *de regimine* are required by the Code to receive this blessing from the bishop of the diocese in which their monastery is situated.[82]

In any case, the abbatial blessing is reserved to the Holy See and in order to administer it, even if selected, the bishop needs a special mandate which must be asked for and received each time an abbot is to be blessed.[83] It is the duty of the new abbot to seek this special mandate for the bishop. A Benedictine abbot need no longer request such a mandate, as a special privilege was granted by Pope Benedict XV whereby this mandate is given to the benedictines *"semel pro semper."* [84]

The phrase *"Abbatum aliasve similes"* used in n. 20 of canon 239, § 1, indicates that any cardinal, even though not endowed with the episcopal character, may impart to the ecclesiastics mentioned in

[80] Cf. Beste, *Introductio in Codicem,* pp. 636-637.

[81] Canon 322, § 2. For a discussion of the various abbots *nullius* and prelates *nullius* who must receive this blessing, the reader is referred to Benko, *The Abbot Nullius,* The Catholic University of America Canon Law Studies, n. 173 (Washington, D. C.: The Catholic University of America Press, 1943), 49-54.

[82] Canon 625.

[83] Benko, *The Abbot Nullius,* p. 56.

[84] Cf. Benko, *loc. cit.*

canons 322, § 2, and 625 the abbatial blessing, ***without the need of the special mandate*** which is required when a bishop imparts this blessing.

The ceremony to be used will be found in the Roman Pontifical. Two distinct ceremonies are given there: the one for the exempt abbots who receive the blessing by papal authority, the other for non-exempt abbots who receive the blessing by episcopal authority. A distinction is also made between a mitred abbot and one who is not mitred. Since the abbot *nullius* is certainly exempt, the first ceremony will be used, and he will be blessed as a mitred abbot, since he is entitled to use the pontifical insignia.[85]

E. *Imparting the Episcopal Blessing to the Faithful.* Section 12 of canon 239, § 1, speaks of the cardinalitial privilege of blessing the faithful after the manner of bishops in any place outside of Rome. The word "*ubique*" used in the canon means that cardinals may impart such a blessing not only in all parts of the world, but is also signifies that the imparting of the blessing is not restricted to the interior of a church or to gatherings of the faithful. In Rome, out of reverence for the Sovereign Pontiff, such an express restriction does apply and as such is contained in the wording of the canon. Outside of Rome, however, a cardinal may impart such a blessing, e. g., while passing through the streets.

The use of the words "*more Episcoporum*" indicates that a cardinal may bless the faithful in the same manner and on the same occasions as a bishop. The occasions, the manner and the form for such blessings are found in the *Pontificale Romanum* and the *Caeremoniale Episcoporum*. But, whereas a bishop is limited to the territory of his jurisdiction in imparting such blessings, a cardinal may impart them anywhere outside of Rome. In Rome, as has been noted, the privilege is restricted to churches, pious places and gatherings of the faithful. A further restriction was placed on this cardinalitial faculty, relative to the four Patriarchal Basilicas of Rome. Under date of May 29, 1934, the Pontifical Commission for the Interpretation of the Code issued a response in which it was stated

[85] Cf. Benko, *op. cit.*, p. 56.

that this faculty (along with those of nn. 12 and 24 of canon 239, § 1) does not extend to the Patriarchal Basilicas of Rome.[36]

Maroto,[37] in explaining this response gives as its basis the fact that basilicas are not comprehended in the term *"ecclesiis."* Even if they were included in the term, the peculiar juridic condition of the Patriarchal Basilicas, which are under the full and immediate jurisdiction and authority of the Roman Pontiff constituting, as it were, his cathedral (St. John Lateran) and co-cathedrals, does not warrant the use of this cardinalitial privilege therein.

Section 2. Faculties in Which Only a Simple Sign of the Cross Need Be Used

Section n. 5 of canon 239, § 1, contains a separate and distinct faculty of blessing various articles and attaching to them the various indulgences that the Holy See is accustomed to attach to such articles, by merely making the sign of the cross over the articles.[38] The list of articles which any cardinal may bless in such a manner is noted taxatively in the faculty.[39] Consequently, this faculty extends only to the articles enumerated in the canon: rosaries, other prayer beads, crosses, medals, statues and scapulars approved by the Holy See. To bless and thereby attach certain specific indulgences to the majority of these articles is reserved to various Religious Orders and Communities. Cardinals receive by this privilege not only the faculty to attach Apostolic Indulgences but also the accumulation of indulgence faculties enjoyed separately by various Religious Orders and Congregations. Simple priests at times may enjoy *some* of these indulgence faculties by way of indult from the Sacred Penitentiary[40] but in attaching the indulgences to the articles covered by their faculty, they ordinarily must use the formula prescribed by the Ritual. The cardinalitial faculty granted by the common law is much more comprehensive than that of any simple

[36] *AAS,* XXVI (1934), 493; Bouscaren, *Digest,* II (1943), 95.

[37] In *Apollinaris,* VIII (1935), 51-54.

[38] Canon 239, § 1, n. 5 is quoted at the beginning of this chapter.

[39] Cf. Toso, *Commentaria,* Lib. II, Tom. II, p. 38.

[40] Cf. decree of March 20, 1933—*AAS,* XXV (1933), 170.

priest. A cardinal may bless these articles ***everywhere, with a simple sign of the cross,*** i.e., he need not use the formula prescribed by the Ritual and ordinarily required for the validity of the blessing.[41] Through the medium of this simple sign of the cross, a cardinal attaches to the article *all* the indulgences that the Holy See is accustomed to attach to such articles.

A. *Rosaries*

There are at least seven different types of prayer beads to which indulgences of various kinds may be attached. The rosary properly so called is the Rosary of the Blessed Virgin Mary, associated with St. Dominic and composed of a set of beads representing a third part of this devotion to the Blessed Virgin. The term *"rosaria"* used in the wording of this cardinalitial privilege refers to these prayer beads associated with St. Dominic.

Very ample indulgences may be gained by the recitation of the rosary without having the beads specially blessed. Whether the beads one uses have been blessed by a Dominican, or by a priest having the faculty to bless them, or whether one uses any beads or not, a person says the rosary of our Lady quite properly and also gains certain indulgences if he says the proper vocal prayers and makes the proper meditations.[42]

In order to attach to a rosary the *full* indulgences conceded by the Church, it is necessary that the article, properly constructed, be blessed by a priest enjoying the faculty and with a prescribed form. Such is the general law for blessing rosaries *and* attaching to them all the indulgences which the Holy See is accustomed to attach.

The first requirement is that the priest have the necessary faculty to attach these indulgences. Now, besides the Apostolic or Papal Indulgences[43] the principal indulgences that the Holy See is

[41] Cf. canon 1148, § 2.

[42] Cf. article by Mutch in *Homiletic and Pastoral Review* (New York, 1900—), XLIII (1942-1943), 429 ff.

[43] The Apostolic or Papal Indulgences are those which, according to a list that the pontiffs are accustomed to promulgate at the beginning of their pontificates, are annexed to articles blessed for that purpose by the Roman Pontiff

accustomed to attach to the rosary are the so-called Dominican, Crosier and Brigittine Indulgences.

The blessing of the Rosary properly so called thereby attaching to it the so-called Dominican Indulgence is proper to the Order of Preachers.[44] This indulgence consists of 100 days for the recitation of each *Pater* and *Ave* on a rosary so blessed. To attach the Crosier Indulgence to the rosary of the Blessed Virgin Mary is proper to the Crosier Fathers. This consists of an indulgence of 500 days for each *Pater* and *Ave* recited while holding a rosary so blessed, whether the entire rosary be said or not. The so-called Brigittine Indulgence is proper to the Order of the Most Holy Saviour. There are ten indulgences comprehended under the general heading of the Brigittine Indulgence. The most familiar of these is that of 100 days indulgence for each *Pater, Ave* and *Credo* recited while holding in the hand a rosary so blessed. The *Credo* is to be recited after every decade of *Aves*. An indulgence of seven years and as many quarantines may be gained by reciting the entire rosary so blessed.[45]

All of the foregoing indulgences are annexed to a rosary when a cardinal merely by making a sign of the cross over the rosary blesses it. No formula is necessary. The simple sign of the cross even without the words that usually accompany it, namely, *"In nomine Patris et Filii et Spiritus Sancti. Amen,"* is sufficient to attach all of the foregoing indulgences to the rosary.

Canon 933 states that many indulgences cannot be gained by one and the same action to which various indulgences have been annexed, unless by special concession of the Holy See some of them may be gained cumulatively. With regard to the rosary, the Holy

or by one who has received the faculty from him. To gain these indulgences it is sufficient to possess articles so blessed, either in one's home or to carry them on one's person and to recite the prescribed prayers. Cf. Fanfani, *De Indulgentiis* (2. ed., Romae, 1926), 92 sq. For the Apostolic Indulgences promulgated by Pius XII, cf. *AAS,* XXXI (1939), 132.

[44] Cf. *Rituale Romanum,* benedictio reservata, n. 35.

[45] Simple priests who are members of the Catholic Near East Welfare Association enjoy the faculty of attaching the Crosier and Brigittine Indulgences to rosaries by a single sign of the cross.

See has made such a special concession. A decision of the Sacred Penitentiary[46] allows the Apostolic and Crosier Indulgences attached to a rosary to be gained by a single recitation of the rosary. It is also allowed to gain the Dominican and the Crosier Indulgences by one and the same recitation of the rosary.

B. *Other Prayer Beads*

As has been mentioned there are at least six other types of prayer beads (*"coronae precatoriae"*) besides the rosary properly so called. Among these are the *Dominican Chaplet* (also called *Corona Domini*). It is not the rosary properly so called, which is usually associated with St. Dominic. Its indulgenced blessing is proper to the Camaldulese Monks. The *Seven Dolor Chaplet* has an indulgenced blessing proper to the Servite Fathers. The *Crosier Chaplet* has an indulgenced blessing proper to the Crosier Fathers. The *Brigittine Chaplet* has an indulgenced blessing proper to the Order of the Most Holy Saviour. The blessing of the *Franciscan Chaplet* is proper to the Franciscans while that of *St. Joseph* is proper to the Carmelites. A final one is the *Angelic Chaplet*.[47]

These and other chaplets of prayer approved by the Holy See may be blessed by any cardinal with a simple sign of the cross, attaching thereto all the indulgences that the Holy See is accustomed to attach to such beads of prayer.

C. *Crosses, Medals and Statues*

The so-called "happy death cross" is a crucifix so blessed that a plenary indulgence (one of the Papal or Apostolic Indulgences) may be gained by anyone who devoutly kisses it at the hour of death. Cardinals may bless and annex to such crucifixes this indulgence by making a simple sign of the cross over it.

The blessings of many medals are reserved to various Religious Communities, e. g., Miraculous Medals and Scapular Medals. To bless the Miraculous Medal and attach to it all the indulgences that the Holy See is accustomed to attach to such medals is a blessing

[46] 14 iun. 1922,—*AAS*, XIV (1922), 394. Cf. also a decree of S. C. de Indulg., 12 iun. 1907,—*ASS*, XL, 442 sq.

[47] Cf. Fanfani, *De Indulgentiis*, p. 121 ff.

proper to the Congregation of the Missions (Vincentian Fathers). The cardinalitial privilege of blessing by a simple sign of the cross extends also to such medals.

The solemn blessing of statues (*"imagines"*) is reserved by the Code to the local Ordinary.[48] All cardinals, however, are privileged to administer this blessing.

D. *Scapulars*

A scapular may be defined as a certain badge or emblem composed of two small pieces of cloth joined together by two small cords, which, out of devotion, is so worn that one piece of cloth reposes on the shoulders and the other hangs upon the breast.[49] There are various species of the scapular. The five principal ones are those of the Most Blessed Trinity, the Immaculate Conception, the Blessed Virgin Mary of Mount Carmel, the Seven Dolors of the Blessed Virgin Mary and that of the Passion of Our Lord Jesus Christ. When blessed and imposed on one of the faithful each of these scapulars carries with it various indulgences.

The blessings of these five scapulars are reserved: that of the Most Blessed Trinity to the Order of the Most Blessed Trinity; that of the Immaculate Conception to the Congregation of Clerics Regular or Theatines; that of the Blessed Virgin Mary of Mount Carmel to the Carmelites; that of the Seven Dolors of the Blessed Virgin Mary to the Servites and that of the Passion of Our Lord to the Passionist Fathers.[50]

Cardinals by a simple sign of the cross may bless these and all other scapulars approved by the Holy See, attaching to them all the indulgences that the Holy See attaches to such scapulars. Moreover, cardinals may impose these scapulars *"sine onere inscriptionis."* If a scapular is the emblem of some confraternity, the person on whom it is imposed must be inscribed in that confraternity. Of the five principal scapulars, those of the Most Blessed Trinity, the Blessed Virgin Mary of Mount Carmel and the Seven Dolors of the

[48] Canon 1279, § 4.

[49] Cf. Fanfani, *De Indulgentiis*, p. 125.

[50] These five scapulars are also known respectively as the white scapular, the blue scapular, the brown scapular and the last two as black scapulars.

Blessed Virgin Mary are emblems of confraternities. Consequently those who wear them must be inscribed in the confraternity by the priest who imposes the scapular. This inscription is necessary for the validity of the imposition.[51] All cardinals in virtue of this privilege are exempted from the requirement of inscribing the name of the person on whom the scapular was imposed in the confraternity.

Pope Pius X (1903-1914) conceded the privilege of substituting in lieu of one or many scapulars approved by the Holy See, a single medal commonly known as the *Scapular Medal,* bearing on one side the Image of our Lord showing His Sacred Heart and on the other an image of the Blessed Virgin Mary.[52] For each species of scapular this medal is to receive the separate respective blessing. These blessings may be imparted, however, by a priest having the necessary faculties with a single sign of the cross.[53]

Since cardinals are privileged to bless both scapulars and medals and attach to them all the indulgences that the Holy See is accustomed to attach to such objects, it follows that by a simple sign of the cross they may bless Scapular Medals and thereby annex to them all the indulgences granted by the Holy See.

This faculty to bless the articles listed above with a simple sign of the cross, is personal to cardinals and therefore cannot be delegated. This is evident from the fact that bishops who enjoy a similar faculty [54] cannot delegate the faculty to priests of their jurisdiction either habitually or even by way of act.[55] Since the Holy See has expressly stated that the similar faculty enjoyed by bishops

[51] Cf. canon 694, § 2. Because of the numerous failures to inscribe such persons the Holy See periodically grants a *sanatio*. The omission of inscription, however, does not deprive a person of the indulgences attached to such a confraternity. (S. Off. [Sect. de Indulg.], 23 apr. 1914—*Fontes,* n. 1295.)

[52] S. Off. (Sect. de Indulg.), 16 dec. 1910,—*AAS,* III (1911), 22.

[53] S. Off., *decret. cit.*; cf. also decrees of S. Off. (Sect. de Indulg.), 5 iun. 1913,—*AAS,* V (1913), 303; 11 maii 1916,—*AAS,* VIII (1916), 175.

[54] Canon 349, § 1, n. 1. Differently from cardinals, bishops must use the prescribed formulas in imparting such blessings; cf. decree of PCI, 12 mar. 1929,—*AAS,* XXI (1929), 170.

[55] S. Poenit., 18 iul. 1919,—*AAS,* XI (1919), 332; 10 nov. 1926,—XVIII (1926), 500. In order to delegate this faculty a bishop must seek a special indult from the Sacred Penitentiary.

as a common law privilege cannot be delegated, it seems to follow *a pari* that cardinals cannot delegate this personal faculty.

There is a further reason to strengthen the assertion that these faculties cannot be delegated by a cardinal. That reason is based on the fact that these faculties concern the concession of certain indulgences and in order that one inferior to the Roman Pontiff may commit to another his faculty of granting indulgences it is required that permission to do so be expressly conceded by the Holy See.[56] No such permission is expressed in this cardinalitial faculty, hence it cannot be delegated.

Section 3. Faculty to Erect and Bless the Stations of the Cross and to Bless Indulgenced Crucifixes of the Via Crucis

Section 6 of canon 239, § 1, states that all cardinals have the faculty to erect the Stations of the Way of the Cross and bless them with a single benediction in any church, oratory (even a private one) and other religious places. They may also bless crucifixes with the indulgences of the Way of the Cross for the benefit of the faithful who through illness or other legitimate impediment are unable to perform this act of devotion in the usual manner.[57]

A. *Stations of the Cross*

The rite of erecting the Stations of the Way of the Cross is a blessing proper to the Franciscan Order of Religious.[58] The rite consists essentially in the blessing of the fourteen wooden crosses, one of which is to be placed above each Station. The indulgences are by direction of the Church attached to the blessed wooden crosses and to no other part of the Stations, no matter how artistic or precious they may be.[59] Previous to 1938 many conditions were

[56] Canon 913.

[57] Cf. canon 239, § 1, n. 6 as quoted at beginning of chapter.

[58] Cf. Appendix of the *Rituale Romanum*.

[59] Cf. *Clergy Review*, XII (1936), 409. Pius XI in a decree issued by the Sacred Penitentiary on October 20, 1931, abrogated all the indulgences which had previously been granted in this matter and promulgated a new list of indulgences that might be gained by this devotion,—*AAS*, XXIII (1931), 522.

attached to this rite affecting its validity.[60] Not infrequently one or the other of these conditions was involuntarily omitted thereby making the erection of the Stations invalid. For that reason it was the custom of the Holy See to grant periodically a general *sanatio.* To prevent such invalid erections of the Stations in the future, Pius XI in 1938[61] abrogated all the conditions that had hitherto been in force and decreed that for the valid erection of the Stations of the Way of the Cross it is sufficient that the priest who is asked to do it have the proper faculty. The exercise of this faculty, however, still seems to be subject to the stipulations of canon 1148, § 2, which states that in blessings and consecrations the formula prescribed by the Church must be used for the validity of the blessing or consecration.

That every cardinal enjoys the proper faculty is evident from section 6 of canon 239, § 1. With regard to its exercise cardinals are further privileged for the faculty states that they may erect the Stations of the Cross *"sub unica benedictione."* This means that without the necessity of following the formula as given in the Roman Ritual, any cardinal may erect the Stations of the Cross by making one sign of the cross over the fourteen wooden crosses.[62] He must, however, recite the usual formula which accompanies the sign of the cross, namely, *"In Nomine Patris et Filii et Spiritus Sancti. Amen."*[63] It is precisely in the recitation of this formula that the phrase *"sub unica benedictione"* differs from the phrase *"solo signo crucis."* The simple sign of the cross without the recitation of the formula that usually accompanies it suffices for the blessings of rosaries, scapulars, etc. It is not sufficient for the blessing and erection of the Stations of the Way of the Cross.

A bishop's faculty in this regard[64] contains the added phrase *"ritibus tamen ab ecclesia praescriptis."* Consequently, a single benediction does not suffice in the case of a bishop's erecting the

60 For these conditions cf. Fanfani, *De Indulgentiis,* p. 115.

61 S. Poenit., *"Iamdiu ac saepe,"* 12 mar. 1938,—*AAS,* XXX (1938), 111.

62 Vermeersch-Creusen, *Epitome,* I (1937), n. 352.

63 Blat, *Commentarium,* II, n. 207.

64 Cf. canon 349, § 1, n. 1.

Stations of the Cross but he must follow the formula given in the Roman Ritual.

This cardinalitial faculty may be exercised in any church, oratory or other pious place even though not an oratory. It is explicitly stated that the faculty extends also to private oratories.

B. *Blessing Crucifixes and Attaching the Indulgences of the Way of the Cross to the Same*

The infirm and others legitimately impeded from performing the Stations of the Cross have from the time of Pope Clement XIV (1769-1774) been granted the privilege of gaining the indulgences of the Way of the Cross by reciting certain prayers and meditating on the Passion while holding in their hand, if possible, a crucifix specially blessed for this purpose.[65] Like the blessing of the Stations of the Cross, the blessing of such a crucifix is proper to the Friars Minor. It has been granted to cardinals also, by a privilege of the common law. In making use of the faculty, however, cardinals are to use the prescribed formula since nothing to the contrary is stated in the faculty.[66]

Just as the faculty for blessing rosaries, scapulars, etc., cannot be delegated to another by a cardinal, so neither may this faculty of erecting and blessing Stations of the Cross and Indulgenced Crucifixes be committed to another. These faculties concern the concession of indulgences and no one under the Roman Pontiff may delegate such a faculty unless permission to do so is expressly contained in the grant of the faculty.[67]

[65] Cf. the following decrees: S. C. Indulg., 8 aug. 1859,—*Decr. Auth. S. C. Ind.*, n. 387; S. Poenit., March 25, 1931,—*AAS*, XXIII (1931), 167; 20 oct. 1931,—*AAS*, XXIII (1931), 522; 9 nov. 1933,—*AAS*, XXV (1933), 502.

[66] Cf. Blat, *Commentarium*, II, n. 207; canon 1148, § 2.

[67] Cf. canon 913. For a cardinal who is also a residential bishop to delegate this faculty either habitually or *per domum actus*, he must seek a special indult from the Holy See. For a priest to erect the Stations of the Cross he must have an indult from the Sacred Penitentiary or provided his bishop has secured the faculty of delegating from the Sacred Penitentiary, he must be delegated by his bishop. Cf. *Ecclesiastical Review* (originally *The American Ecclesiastical Review*, Philadelphia, 1889-1944; Washington, D. C., 1944—), XCVIII (1938), 175, 566-569.

CHAPTER VIII

PRIVILEGES THAT CONCERN THE CONCESSION AND GAINING OF CERTAIN INDULGENCES

An indulgence is defined as the remission before God of all or part of the temporal punishment due for sins whose guilt has already been forgiven. This remission is conceded by ecclesiastical authority from the treasury of the Church, for living persons by way of absolution, for the dead by way of suffrage.[1]

Not only as the beneficiaries of indulgences do cardinals enjoy certain common law privileges, but what is more important, they are constituted by way of privilege as competent ministers of the jurisdictional act of granting certain specific indulgences.

Article I. Privileges That Concern the Granting of Indulgences

Canon 239, § 1, n. 24: Concedendi indulgentias ducentorum dierum, etiam toties quoties lucrandas, in locis vel institutis ac pro personis suae iurisdictionis vel protectionis; item in aliis locis, sed a praesentibus solummodo, singulis vicibus, lucrandas.

As has been noted in the definition given above, when the Church grants an indulgence she withdraws from an inexhaustible storehouse of satisfactions, known as the treasury of the Church, some part of the wealth there stored and places it at the disposal of him who gains the indulgence. This the gainer may offer to God in lieu of the actual endurance of the temporal punishment which he owes because of his sins. The "*thesaurus ecclesiae*" is composed of the infinite satisfactions of Christ, the abundant satisfactions of the Blessed Mother of God and those of the Saints. These were stored

[1] Canon 911.

away, so to speak, for future emergencies, to be applied at a later time in expiating the penalties due to the sins of generations to come.[2]

The disposal of this rich treasure has been entrusted to the authority of the Catholic Church.[3] This power to grant indulgences is but one phase of the power given to the Church "to bind and to loose," the power of the keys entrusted to St. Peter and his successors, the Roman Pontiffs. Being one aspect of the power of the keys, the granting of indulgences for the faithful is an act of jurisdiction.[4] Therefore, it is to be exercised by the ecclesiastical authority to whom Christ has committed jurisdiction over the faithful, to whose keeping has been entrusted the treasury of the Church. Consequently, the Pope alone, as the Vicar of Christ, has the primary and supreme power over the concession of indulgences. Other than the Holy Father, no one can grant indulgences by ordinary power except those to whom such power is expressly conceded by the law.[5] Even when such power is conceded to one inferior to the Roman Pontiff, the law imposes certain restrictions on the use of that power. These restrictions are enumerated in canon 913.

First among the several classes of persons to whom such power is conceded by the law are cardinals.[6] By the law of the Code cardinals are empowered to grant indulgences of 200 days. Recently, however, this faculty has been enlarged to 300 days by Pope Pius XII in recognition of the solicitude and good wishes in his behalf on the occasion of his twenty-fifth anniversary in the episcopate.[7]

With regard to the historical background of this privilege it may be noted that in earlier times cardinals enjoyed in and for their title churches the faculty of granting indulgences of 100 days.[8]

[2] Cf. Hagedorn, *General Legislation on Indulgences,* The Catholic University of America Canon Law Studies, n. 22 (Washington, D. C.: The Catholic University of America, 1924), p. 54; hereafter cited *Indulgences.*

[3] Cf. canon 911.

[4] Cf. Fanfani, *De Indulgentiis,* n. 5, p. 11.

[5] Canon 912.

[6] Canon 239, § 1, n. 24 as quoted at beginning of this article.

[7] Cf. Decree of Sacred Penitentiary, July 20, 1942—*AAS,* XXXIV (1942), 240.

[8] Cf. *above,* Chapter I, Article IV, p. 12.

Diana (1586-1663) expressly maintained that this faculty was one of the privileges enjoyed in virtue of custom rather than by written grant.[9] In 1903 the Sacred Congregation of Indulgences issued a decree permitting cardinals to grant indulgences of 200 days both in their titles and dioceses.[10] Even at this time the faculty was restricted to places under a cardinal's jurisdiction, namely, to his title church and, if he was also a residential bishop, to his diocese.

The legislation of the Code as modified by the decree of 1942 permit all cardinals, even those not bishops, the right of granting indulgences of 300 days not only in places and for persons under their jurisdiction, but also in places over which they have no jurisdiction whatever.

This power of granting indulgences, as has been noted, is an exercise of jurisdiction and even though it is enjoyed by cardinals through a privilege, it is nevertheless ordinary jurisdiction.[11] The fact that it is annexed to the cardinalitial office by way of privilege, in no way militates against its being ordinary jurisdiction, for the privilege by which it is so annexed is a privilege of the common law. The power is therefore annexed to the office *ipso iure*.

Though it is ordinary power,[12] it cannot be delegated to others, for canon 913, n. 1, expressly states that the faculty of granting indulgences enjoyed by one inferior to the Roman Pontiff cannot be committed to others unless express permission to do so has been granted by the Holy See.

Another restriction placed on this cardinalitial faculty of granting indulgences is that a cardinal cannot grant indulgences applicable to the souls in purgatory.[13] Consequently, the beneficiaries

[9] *Resolutiones Morales*, Vol. V, tom. 9, tract. 7, res. 46.

[10] *Urbis et orbis*, 28 aug. 1903: "Quapropter Sanctitas Sua, percepta omnium relatione, non modo memoratis votis annuere, verum etiam, clementer decernere dignata est ut in posterum Emi. Patres Cardinales, in suis titulis aeque ac dioecesibus, bis centum . . . dierum indulgentiam elargiri valeant, dum tamen serventur cuncta huc usque ab eisdem servata in huiusmodi indulgentiarum elargitionibus."—*ASS*, XXXVI (1903-1904), 318.

[11] Cf. Hagedorn, *op. cit.*, p. 73.

[12] Canon 912.

[13] Canon 913, n. 2: Inferiores Romano Pontifice nequeunt: indulgentias concedere defunctis applicabiles.

of indulgences granted by cardinals can be only living members of the Church.

In the faculty itself definite conditions for the gaining of these cardinalitial indulgences are set forth. In places or institutes under a cardinal's jurisdiction or protection *and* by persons under such jurisdiction or protection, these indulgences may be gained *"toties quoties."* The term *"toties quoties"* applied to an indulgence signifies that an indulgence so conceded may be gained as many times even on one and the same day as the enjoined acts (e. g., the visitation of a church, certain prayers, etc.) are repeated.[14] Indulgences to be gained in this manner may be granted by a cardinal only in places or institutes under his jurisdiction or protection; they may be gained *"toties quoties"* only by persons who are subject to this jurisdiction or protection. Thus for instance, in the church assigned to him as titular a cardinal may attach an indulgence of 300 days to visiting a certain statue. Such an indulgence may be gained by the faithful belonging to that parish as often as the visit is made. Or, the cardinal-protector of a certain Religious Order or Congregation [15] may concede an indulgence of 300 days to the members of that Religious group for saying certain specified prayers. Such an indulgence could be gained as many times as the specified prayers

[14] Cf. Fanfani, *De Indulgentiis,* n. 3, p. 8.

[15] Cf. canon 499, § 2. St. Francis of Assisi said in his rule (Chapter XII): "I command the Ministers in obedience to ask of the Lord Pope one of the Cardinals of the Holy Roman Church as governor, protector, and corrector of this Fraternity." Other Orders followed the example of St. Francis and it became the general practice for religious Orders to have a cardinal-protector. In recent times also Congregations of pontifical right usually ask for a protector. The extensive powers enjoyed by the Cardinal Protector in former times were reduced by Pope Innocent XII (1691-1700) in his Constitution *"Christi Fidelium,"* February 16, 1694 (*Bull. Rom.*, XX, 594 sq.) to a general paternal interest in the welfare of the respective organization. The legislation of canon 499, § 2 is fundamentally based on that constitution. Cf: Woywod, *A Practical Commentary on the Code of Canon Law* (Revised by Rev. Callistus Smith, 2 vols., New York: Joseph F. Wagner, Inc., 1943), I, pp. 184-185. Cardinals were also appointed as protectors of Pious Institutions and Christian Nations. For the history of cardinal-protectors up to the sixteenth century, cf. Plati (1548-1591), *De Dignitate et Officio Cardinalis* (6. ed., Romae, 1836), pp. 362-374.

were recited. Finally, if a cardinal is also a residential bishop or archbishop having a diocese under his jurisdiction, he may grant indulgences of 300 days throughout his diocese and even for churches pertaining to exempt religious.[16] Because he is also a bishop or archbishop, the indulgences granted by such a cardinal may be gained *"toties quoties"* not only by his subjects as allowed for cardinalitial indulgences by canon 239, but also, unless he has stated otherwise, by *peregrini, vagi* and all exempt persons who are actually staying in the diocese.[17]

In all other places outside the realm of his jurisdiction or protection, a cardinal may grant an indulgence of 300 days. Such indulgences, however, may not be gained *"toties quoties,"* but are subject to definite limitations. These may be gained once only, and only by those present at the time of the concession. A cardinal may grant such an indulgence in any part of the world. In Rome, however, the faculty may not be used in the four Patriarchal Basilicas. This exception was decreed by the Pontifical Commission for the Interpretation of the Code on May 29, 1934.[18]

As has been noted in speaking of other privileges which may not be exercised in the patriarchal basilicas, the reason for this exception is based on the peculiar juridic position of these four basilicas which constitute, as it were, the cathedral (St. John Lateran) and co-cathedrals of the Roman Pontiff. As such they are under the immediate jurisdiction of the Holy Father. Hence, no one, not even a cardinal, without the permission of the Pontiff himself, may perform any act that even hints of jurisdiction in these basilicas.[19] The act of granting indulgences is definitely an act of jurisdiction. For this reason, therefore, a cardinal may not make use of his privilege of granting indulgences in the four patriarchal basilicas.

[16] Cf. response of Pontifical Commission for the interpretation of the Code under date of December 6, 1930,—*AAS,* XXIII (1931), 25.

[17] Canon 927: Nisi aliud ex concessionis tenore appareat, indulgentias ab Episcopo concessas lucrari possunt tum subditi extra territorium, tum peregrini, vagi, omnesque exempti in territorio degentes.

[18] Cf. *AAS,* XXVI (1934), 493.

[19] Cf. Maroto, "Commentarium in Responsum P.C.I. ad Can. 239, § 1, nn. 12, 13, 14,"—*Apollinaris,* VIII (1935), 51-54.

That this cardinalitial faculty of granting indulgences throughout the world fully partakes of the nature of a privilege is quite evident when one considers that the granting of indulgences implies jurisdiction. Now, ordinarily an act of jurisdiction may be directly exercised only over one's proper subjects.[20] In view of that fact the common law has stipulated that ecclesiastical superiors inferior to the Roman Pontiff may directly grant indulgences only to their immediate subjects.[21] However, since indulgences are favors granted by the Church, and that their privileged character might appear to advantage, the Church has modified the expression *"subject of the grantor."* It is declared in the Code that subjects while outside the diocese, visitors to the diocese with a domicile elsewhere and those in the diocese who have no domicile whatever, as well as exempt religious sojourning in the diocese may gain indulgences granted by the bishop unless the terms of the concession exclude such persons.[22]

Such are the stipulations of the general law relative to the beneficiaries of the jurisdictional act of granting indulgences. Cardinals, however, in virtue of their privilege are exempted from this general legislation, for it is expressly stated that they may grant indulgences of 300 days *everywhere,* i. e., even outside of places subject to their jurisdiction or protection.

Article II. Privileges That Concern the Gaining of Certain Indulgences

The Church grants indulgences, not as absolute and free gifts, but as contingent concessions dependent on the performance of certain works as conditions *sine qua non.*[23] Among the conditions usually imposed in the concession of very many indulgences is a visit to a church or public oratory. This condition is sometimes joined with other conditions, but often is prescribed as the only condition necessary for the gaining of the indulgence.

[20] Cf. canon 201, § 1.

[21] Canon 925, § 1: Ut quis sit capax sibi lucrandi indulgentias, debet esse baptizatus, non excommunicatus, in statu gratiae saltem in fine operum praescriptorum, *subditum concedentis.* (Italics are the writer's.)

[22] Canon 927; Hagedorn, *Indulgences,* p. 84.

[23] Cf. Hagedorn, *Indulgences,* p. 100.

Until 1933 the exact meaning and force of the clause "to visit a church or public oratory" had been the subject of considerable dispute. Because of these disputes the Sacred Penitentiary under date of September 20, 1933,[24] stated that Pius XI "in order to remove all doubt and future anxiety graciously deigned to declare: that by a visit to a church or oratory is meant 'going to a church or oratory at least with some general or implicit intention of honoring God in Himself or in His saints, and making some prayer, the one prescribed if any has been imposed by the one who granted the indulgence, otherwise, any prayer, oral or even mental, according to each one's piety and devotion.' "[25]

In some indulgences the visit prescribed is to some determined church or oratory, not merely to any one. Thus, the Portiuncula Indulgence is granted for visiting a church of the Franciscans or another church that enjoys the Portiuncula privilege.[26]

Cardinals together with the members of their households are the recipients of a special privilege relative to gaining those indulgences to which is annexed the condition of a visit to a church or oratory. Section 11 of canon 239, § 1, states that all cardinals and the members of their households enjoy the privilege of gaining in their own private chapels those indulgences for which a visit to some temple or public shrine is prescribed in the town or city in which a cardinal is actually sojourning. This privilege seems to be new with the Code.

The privilege envisages only *local indulgences,* i. e., those which are immediately attached to a pious place (as a church, oratory or

[24] *AAS,* XXV (1933), 446.

[25] English translation is taken from Bouscaren, *Digest,* I, 458.

[26] This indulgence in honor of St. Francis of Assisi and the Chapel of the Portiuncula in Assisi, is a plenary indulgence granted by the Roman Pontiff to be gained *"toties quoties"* by visiting on the second day of August any Franciscan Church or Oratory, or other churches that have obtained the privilege of the Portiuncula from the Sacred Penitentiary, and saying at each visit at least six *Paters, Aves* and *Glorias* according to the intention of the Holy Father. For various decrees concerning this indulgence cf. *AAS,* XVI (1924), 345; XXII (1930), 43; XXXI (1939), 226. In the Chapel of the Portiuncula at Assisi and in the Basilica of St. Peter in Rome this indulgence may be gained every day of the year. (Cf. Fanfani, *De Indulgentiis,* p. 18.)

chapel).[27] Consequently, wherever a cardinal is actually sojourning, whether in Rome or outside of Rome, he and his "*familiares*" [28] may gain by visiting the cardinal's private chapel any such local indulgences to which is annexed as a condition *sine qua non* a visit to a church or oratory. Since the canon uses the words "*templi alicuius vel publicae aediculae,*" the significance is that even if the visit prescribed is to some determined church or shrine, cardinals and their *familiares* may still gain the indulgence by a visit to the cardinal's private chapel.[29]

From the wording of the privilege, it appears that the city, town or village in which the cardinal is at the moment residing either permanently or only for a short time, e. g., when on a trip, will determine the type of local indulgences that may be gained by a visit to the cardinal's private chapel. The private chapel as mentioned in the canon refers either to the chapel in the cardinal's permanent residence or to a private chapel that he is making use of, e. g., when on a trip.

The following schema will indicate the various local indulgences that a cardinal and the members of his household may gain.

A. *In the Chapel of a Cardinal's Permanent Residence:*

(a) All local indulgences that require a visit to *any* church or public oratory anywhere in the world.

(b) All local indulgences that require a visit to *any* church or public oratory of *that* city or town.

(c) All local indulgences that require a visit to *a determined* church, oratory or shrine of *that* city or town.

B. *In a Chapel being Used by a Cardinal when away from his Permanent Residence:*

(a) All local indulgences that require a visit to *any* church or public oratory *anywhere* in the world.

[27] Cf. Fanfani, *De Indulgentiis,* n. 3; Hagedorn, *Indulgences,* pp. 69-70.

[28] For a determination of the various persons comprehended in this term, cf. *above,* p. 58.

[29] Cf. Blat, *Commentarium,* II, n. 211; Fanfani, *De Indulgentiis,* n. 41, p. 48.

(b) All local indulgences that require a visit to *any* church or public oratory of *that* city or town (in which the cardinal is sojourning at the moment).

(c) All local indulgences that require a visit to *a determined* church, oratory or shrine of *that* city or town (in which the cardinal is sojourning at the moment).

Finally, it is to be noted that the mere physical visitation of the cardinal's private chapel does not suffice to gain such an indulgence. The visitation must be accompanied by some general or implicit intention of honoring God in Himself or in His Saints, and by some prayer, the one prescribed if any has been imposed by the one who granted the indulgence, otherwise, any prayer, oral or mental, according to each one's piety and devotion.[30]

[30] S. Poenit., 20 sept. 1933,—*AAS,* XXV (1933), 446.

CHAPTER IX

PRIVILEGES THAT CONCERN EXEMPTIONS IN JUDICIAL PROCEDURE AND PENAL LEGISLATION

Article I. Privileges of Exemption in Judicial Procedure

A judiciary department is a necessary requisite of every perfect society that the laws governing its members be properly interpreted, applied and carried out. This is a fundamental principle of jurisprudence. Both Church and State as perfect societies are entitled to maintain their separate judiciary systems to vindicate the private rights of their individual members as well as the common good of the society against delinquent members.[1]

To govern the functioning of its judiciary department the Church has enacted definite legislation. This procedural legislation contained in Book IV of the Code of Canon Law, like that of every judiciary system, exists primarily for the fundamental purpose of determining and safeguarding the rights of a plaintiff and of a defendant in such matters. The plaintiff and defendant constitute the focal point of procedural legislation, and the determination and protection of their rights constitute the ultimate aim and object of a judicial process.[2]

The first step in any judicial process is to determine that the matter involved in a definite case is such as comes within the competence or jurisdictional limits of the tribunal. From earliest times the Church has asserted its right to judge exclusively all cases, civil or ecclesiastical, contentious or criminal, of persons who enjoy the *privilegium fori.*[3]

[1] Cf. Cappello, *Summa Iuris Publici Ecclesiastici* (4. ed., Romae: Universitas Gregoriana, 1936), pp. 68-72, 76-79; Dugan, *The Judiciary Department of the Diocesan Curia,* The Catholic University of America Canon Law Studies, n. 26 (Washington, D. C.: The Catholic University of America, 1925), pp. 12-14.

[2] Cf. Król, *The Defendant in Contentious Trials,* The Catholic University of America Canon Law Studies, n. 146 (Washington, D. C.: The Catholic University of America Press, 1942), Foreword.

[3] Cf. canon 1552, § 1, n. 3.

Section 1. The Special Privilegium Fori of Cardinals.

The ***privilegium fori*** consists in the exemption of all members of the clergy, religious of either sex and novices, and members of pious societies who live in common without vows, from the power and jurisdiction of secular or civil tribunals.[4] It is a specification of the Church's doctrine of clerical immunity.[5] The strict ***privilegium fori*** as enunciated in the Code rules that it is forbidden to convene clerics before a civil tribunal without the permission of their competent ecclesiastical superior, unless some other provisions have been legitimately made for particular places.[6] It is in the matter of the competent ecclesiastical superior from whom such permission must be sought that the cardinalitial privilege is mentioned. No cardinal may be convened before a civil tribunal unless the plaintiff has first received the permission of the Holy See.[7] This prohibition is sanctioned by an ***ipso facto*** excommunication reserved ***speciali modo*** to the Holy See.[8] Such is the special extension of the ***privilegium fori*** enjoyed by cardinals.

[4] Canon 1553, § 1, n. 3.

[5] ***Materially,*** clerical immunity is the sum of exemptions from the secular power which the Church accords to clerics and religious. ***Formally,*** it is a ***jus singulare*** which clerics enjoy by right and religious by extension, established by the Church and consisting of their exemption from the jurisdiction of civil courts and from other obligations and duties commonly imposed by the State upon citizens. This doctrine is, as it were, a chapter in the more extensive history of the relations of Church and State. It is a corollary and exemplification of the broader concept of the liberty and independence of the Church from secular interference. For a complete study of the history and juridical origin of the doctrine of clerical immunity, the reader is referred to Downs, ***The Concept of Clerical Immunity,*** The Catholic University of America Canon Law Studies, n. 126, Washington, D. C.: The Catholic University of America Press, 1941, hereafter cited ***Clerical Immunity.***

[6] Canon 120, § 1: Clerici in omnibus causis sive contentiosis sive criminalibus apud iudicem ecclesiasticum conveniri debent, nisi aliter pro locis particularibus legitime provisum fuerit.

[7] Canon 120, § 2: Patres Cardinales, Legati Sedis Apostolicae, Episcopi etiam titulares, Abbates vel Praelati ***nullius,*** supremi religionum iuris pontificii superiores, Officiales maiores Romanae Curiae, of negotia ad ipsorum munus pentinentia, apud iudicem laicum conveniri nequeunt sine venia Sedis Apostolicae; . . .

[8] Cf. canon 2341.

The doctrine of the privileged forum was much more rigorously set forth in earlier times. Civil authorities, however, did not always recognize it and often openly opposed it, especially following the Protestant Reformation and the French Revolution. In order to defend herself against such actions by the secular power and to seek *a modus vivendi* between Church and State, the Church has at times found it necessary to enter into concordats with various nations, allowing concessions which amounted to a validation of what had been usurpations by the civil power.[9] The phrase *"nisi aliter pro locis particularibus legitime provisum fuerit"* of canon 120, § 1, has especial reference to such concordats. In the United States, as in many other countries, the civil government has never recognized the privileged forum of clerics. Because of this attitude, the Third Plenary Council of Baltimore forbade priests to sue other ecclesiastics in civil courts without the written permission of the bishop.[10] However, this same Council, by its silence on the question, implicitly recognized and authorized the custom prevailing in the United States in virtue of which laymen could bring clerics before the civil courts without first having consulted the bishop. This custom has not been abrogated by the Code, for canon 120, § 1, allows for certain legislative customs in the phrase *"nisi aliter pro locis particularibus provisum fuerit."*[11]

In 1928, however, a decree came forth from Rome in which it was stated that certain American laymen had incurred the *ipso facto* excommunication of canon 2341 for convening their Ordinary, Bishop W. Hickey of Providence, R. I., before a civil tribunal without first having sought the permission of the Holy See.[12]

[9] Cf. Downs, *Clerical Immunity*, p. 33.

[10] *Acta et Decreta Concilii Plenarii Baltimorensis Tertii* (Baltimorae, 1886), n. 84.

[11] Cf. Burke, *Competence in Ecclesiastical Tribunals*, The Catholic University of America Canon Law Studies, n. 14 (Washington, D. C.: The Catholic University of America, 1922), p. 83; Barrett, *A Comparative Study of the Councils of Baltimore and the Code of Canon Law*, The Catholic University of America Canon Law Studies, n. 83 (Washington, D. C.: The Catholic University of America, 1932), pp. 33-37.

[12] *AAS*, XX (1928), 146. The case was that of E. J. Daignault of Woonsocket, R. I., vs. W. Hickey, Bishop of Providence, R. I

In view of this decree a distinction must be made concerning the custom that prevailed in the United States prior to the Code and after the Code. With regard to the privileged forum of *minor ecclesiastics,* it may be maintained that the phrase *"nisi aliter pro locis particularibus legitime provisum fuerit"* of canon 120, § 1 allows for the custom, tacitly approved by the Third Plenary Council of Baltimore, in virtue of which laymen may bring such minor ecclesiastics before civil tribunals without first seeking the permission of the bishop. With regard to the privileged forum of *major ecclesiastics,* such as cardinals, and bishops, however, it must be maintained that in view of the decree of 1928, the *nisi* clause of canon 120, § 1 provides only for exceptions permitted by concordats; it cannot be said to provide for any customs derogatory to the privileged forum of such major ecclesiastics.

Such a distinction seems to be legitimate in view of the fact that the Holy See itself has definitely distinguished the privileged forum of major ecclesiastics from that of minor ecclesiastics by constituting distinct sources from which the necessary permissions are to be obtained, as well as distinct punishments by which violations of the privileged fora of these two types of clerics are punished.[13] Downs leaves room for such a distinction in his assertion that "it is to be observed that the present law contains no clause which would reprobate a contrary custom against clerical immunity. . . . Granted that tacit toleration of customs derogatory to be clerical immunity in order to avoid greater evils does *not necessarily* and in all cases amount to tacit consent, nevertheless, in some cases it may amount to such."[14] In speaking directly of the decree of 1928, Downs observes, "the excommunication . . . indicates that the view cannot be held that custom has *completely* abolished the privileged forum in the United States.[15] Following Downs, the writer maintains that tacit consent has been accorded the custom existing in the United States derogatory to the privileged forum of minor ecclesiastics, but that no custom may be tolerated against the privileged forum of cardinals and other major ecclesiastics.

[13] Cf. canon 2341.

[14] *Clerical Immunity,* p. 50.

[15] *Loc. cit.* (Italics are the writer's.)

In view of this cardinalitial privilege, no cardinal may be called before a secular judge as a defendant [16] in any type of case whether temporal or spiritual, criminal or contentious.[17] unless permission has been obtained previously from the Holy See. By the force of this privilege even the temporal cases in which cardinals are concerned as defendants are reserved to the competency of ecclesiastical tribunals.

It is evidenced from facts that modern states no longer recognize the privileged forum even for such illustrious ecclesiastics as cardinals, for, prior to the Lateran Pact, there were instances of cardinals being summoned to appear before civil tribunals even in Rome. Augustine,[18] mentions the Verdesi-Bricardelli case, in which certain

[16] The word *"conveniri"* used in canon 120, signifies: *"in iudicium vocare seu comparere facere ut reum, et quidem in propria persona et suo nomine."* Cf. Beste, *Introductio in Codicem,* p. 177. Therefore, a cardinal could be called as a witness, an expert or as an administrator of some moral personality. Cf. Vermeersch-Creusen, *Epitome,* I, n. 242; Toso, *Commentaria,* Lib. II, Tom. I, p. 75.

[17] Temporal cases are especially comprehended under this privilege. Purely ecclesiastical cases are not directly envisaged, for in them clerics and lay people alike are subject to ecclesiastical authority alone. The cases comprehended in the *privilegium fori,* are those that are temporal in themselves (e. g., contentious cases that concern wills, inheritances or property, etc., as well as all criminal cases of secular law), which because of their connection with the person of a cleric, acquire a certain spiritual aspect. Cf. Burke, *Competence in Ecclesiastical Tribunals,* p. 76. Moreover, canon 120, § 2 does not intend to limit this privilege of cardinals only to *"negotia ad ipsorum munus pertinentia."* That phrase refers only to the personalities immediately preceding it, namely, *"Officiales maiores Romanae Curiae, ob negotia ad ipsorum munus pertinentia."* The comma separating the phrase from the group of personalities preceding it would seem to indicate that the phrase has reference to all the dignitaries mentioned. Such an interpretation cannot be justified in view of the structure of canon 2341 wherein the punishment for plaintiffs who violate canon 120, §§ 1 and 2 is stated. The same wording is used in canon 2341 but without the disturbing comma, making it evident that the phrase refers only to the major officials of the Roman Curia. Besides, it would be illogical to refer the phrase to all the personalities that precede it, for titular bishops, who have no munus, are included. Cf. Blat, *Commentarium,* II, n. 56; Vermeersch-Creusen, *Epitome,* I, n. 242; Toso, *Commentaria,* Lib. II, Tom. I, p. 77; Beste, *Introductio,* p. 177.

[18] *Commentary,* II, p. 61.

cardinals were cited to appear in civil court and were excused only on the ground that exemption was attached to the royal order of the Annunziata to which the cardinals happened to belong. Such an incident, however, instead of weakening the Church's stand on clerical immunity, was the occasion of the famous Motu proprio of Pius X, *Quantavis diligentia,* of October 9, 1911.[19]

The insistence of the Church on her doctrine of clerical immunity and in particular on the exemption of clerics from secular jurisdiction is evidenced in the Code from the severe punishments with which she sanctions any violations of her stand.[20] The Church thereby wishes to defend her doctrine against all encroachments of the secular powers other than those she permits by concordats and legitimate custom.

Section 2. Contentious and Criminal Trials of Cardinals Are Reserved to the Exclusive and Personal Competence of the Pope.

Once the Church had established the exclusive competence of ecclesiastical tribunals in all cases, temporal or ecclesiastical, of clerics, the next step in the procedural legislation of the Church was to set forth norms governing the competence of the various ecclesiastical tribunals. This she has done in canons 1556-1568.

Competency refers to that definite jurisdiction by which a certain judge or tribunal is empowered to judge a specific case of certain individuals in a determined territory. It is variously determined according to the persons involved in the suit, the nature of the case and the territorial district within which the defendant has a domicile or quasi-domicile.[21]

Any case that involves a cardinal, whether it be contentious or criminal,[22] is reserved in the procedural legislation of the Church to

[19] *AAS,* III (1911), 555; Ayrinhac held that this decree did not refer to the long-standing contrary custom of the United States. Cf. "The Motu Proprio 'Quantavis Diligentia'"—*AER,* XLVII (1912), 303-315.

[20] Cf. canon 2341.

[21] Cf. Burke, *Competence in Ecclesiastical Tribunals,* p. 6 ff.

[22] Canon 1552, § 2: Obiectum iudicii sunt: personarum physicarum vel moralium iura persequenda aut vindicanda, vel earundem personarum facta

the exclusive and personal competence of the Roman Pontiff.[23] Such cases are *causae maiores*.[24] Consequently, in view of the *privilegium fori*, any case that involves a cardinal, whether it is concerned with temporal matters or strictly ecclesiastical matters, is to be judged even in the first instance exclusively by the Roman Pontiff.[25] Since every other judge or tribunal is absolutely incompetent to judge such cases,[26] the sentence rendered by an inferior judge or tribunal who would accept and judge the case of a cardinal, would be vitiated by an irremediable nullity.[27]

This privilege accorded cardinals because of their illustrious dignity is by no means new with the Code. An example cited in decretal legislation is that of a case handled by Boniface VIII (1294-1303). In a decretal letter Boniface mentioned the case of two notorious cardinals, James and Peter Colonna, whom he himself had deposed as schismatics because of their unwillingness to render obedience to the canonically elected pontiff and their continued rebellion against the duly constituted Church authorities. Boniface himself, as the letter indicates, had judged the case and inflicted the punishments.[28]

iuridica declaranda; et tunc iudicium est *contentiosum*; delicta in ordine ad poenam infligendam vel declarandam; et tunc iudicium est *criminale*.

[23] Canon 1557, § 1, n. 2: Ipsius Romani Pontificis dumtaxat ius est iudicandi: Patres Cardinales.

[24] Canon 220: Gravoris momenti negotia quae uni Romano Pontifici reservantur sive natura sua, sive positiva lege, *causae maiores appellantur*.

[25] Coronata notes that the Supreme Pontiff may be a special delegation remit these cases of cardinals to others to draw them up or even to judge them. (*Institutiones*, III [Torino, 1933]), p. 11, nota (4) ad calcem.

[26] Canon 1558: In causis de quibus in can. 1556, 1557, aliorum iudicum incompetentia est *absoluta*.

[27] Canon 1892, n. 1: Sententia vitio insanabilis nullitatis laborat, quando: lata est a iudice absolute incompetente. . . .

[28] C. un., *de schismaticis*, V, 3 in VI°: " . . . *Processus* tamen *contra ipsos* et alios *fecimus* successive varios, diversisque temporibus spirituales et temporales poenas et sententias continentes et mulctas. . . . (He then mentions the punishments he had inflicted.) . . . Haec et alia *per nos facta* in praedictis *nostris processibus* . . . confirmamus et innovamus. . . ." (Italics are the writer's.) This letter was issued on Ascension Thursday, 1297,—Potthast, n. 24520.

In his celebrated constitution on the dignity of the cardinalate[29] Eugene IV (1431-1447) declared: *"S.R.E. Cardinales, a nemine, nisi a Romano Pontifice iudicentur."*

Riganti[30] cites many examples taken from the pontificates of Eugene IV, Julius II (1503-1513) and Pius IV (1559-1565) in which these pontiffs personally judged the cases of cardinals. Riganti[31] quotes an excerpt from a letter sent by Pius IV to the French Cardinal, Charles de Guise of Lorraine, concerning the process of deposition that had been carried out in Rome against another Frenchman, Cardinal de Châtillon, the brother of Admiral de Coligny, leader of the Hugenots. It seems that certain French Officials considered this a violation of the French Concordat.[32] To inform the French officials in question that no competence to judge the *causae maiores* of cardinals had been granted in the French Concordat, Pius IV wrote as follows:

> "*. . . quod ad acta iudicialia adversus Castilioneum et alios episcopos edita spectat, pro explorato habeat, nil actum contra constitutiones Regni Galliae, quia Cardinalium et Episcoporum causae reservatae sunt Pontifici ex ipsis Concordatis cum Galliae Regibus, causaeque maiores et graviores semper Sedi Apostolicae reservantur. . . .*"

[29] *"Non mediocri"* (a. 1439), § 14,—*Fontes*, n. 50.

[30] *Commentaria in Regulas, Constitutiones et Ordinationes Cancellariae Apostolicae* (4 vols. in 2, Coloniae Allobrogum, 1751), III, in Reg. XXXVII, nn. 143-180 (hereafter cited as *Commentaria*); cf. also, Albanus, *De Cardinalatu*, quest. XLII, p. XCVII; Germonius, *De Indultis Apostolicis*, p. 6, n. 8.

[31] *Ibidem*, n. 180.

[32] Because secular powers often refused to recognize certain rights of the Church, e. g., the privileged forum of clerics, the Holy See, as a *modus vivendi* between Church and State, found it necessary to enter into pacts or concordats with various nations. In these the Holy See *in practice* allowed concessions which in fact amounted to a validation of what had been usurpations by the civil power; and was content to accept guarantees for the preservation of the dignity of clerics in their arrest, detention, conviction and punishment by the civil governments for offenses against the civil law. Cf. Downs, *Clerical Immunity*, pp. 33-37. The French Concordat was confirmed by Pope Leo X (1513-1521) on August 16, 1516. Cf. Fifth Lateran Council, sess. 11,—Mansi, *Sacrorum Conciliorum, Nova et Amplissima Collectio* (53 vols. in 59, Parisiis, 1901-1927), XXXII, 947 (hereafter cited as Mansi).

Pope Paul IV (1555-1559) who had immediately preceded Pius IV as the Roman Pontiff had expressly reserved to himself all cases in which the litigants were cardinals, i. e. cases in which one cardinal was the plaintiff and another the defendant.[83]

The pre-Code legislation on this cardinalitial privilege has been succinctly summed up by Riganti in the following passage: [84]

> *"Cardinalium causas supremo Romani Pontificis iudicio tantummodo definiendas esse, quaeque locum sibi vindicat, etiamsi ab Urbe ipsos abesse contingat, quia nempe S.R.E. Cardinales maxima excellunt dignitate post Summum Pontificem, ac sequiparantur Illustribus seu Senatoribus, et clarissimis Viris, unde summopere decet ut non ab aliis iudicentur, quam a Papa, cujus corporis partes sunt."*

The exclusive competence of the Roman Pontiff over such cases as enunciated in canon 1557 of the Code is merely a confirmation of the pre-Code procedural legislation on this point.

Section 3. Privileges Enjoyed When Acting As Witnesses in Ecclesiastical Trials

The Code rules that ordinarily witnesses are to be examined in the place where court is held.[85] This prescription the Church has taken over from the Roman Law enactment of the Emperor Justinian (527-565).[86] Cardinals, however, when acting as witnesses, because of their eminent dignity are accorded the privilege of selecting the place in which they desire to make their depositions. Upon

[83] Motu propr., *"Cum saepius,"* 9 ian. 1556: "... omnes et singulos lites et causas inter quoscumque S.R.E. Cardinales super quibusvis rebus et bonis, tam ecclesiasticis quam saecularibus . . . vel attentatis aut innovatis coram quibusvis iudicibus, etiam eiusdem S.R.E. Cardinalibus aut Palatii Apostolici causarum Auditoribus, in quavis instantia ac etiam in negotio exequutivo . . . pro expressis haberi volumus, ad nos in eisdem statu et terminis in quibus reperiuntur advocamus, cognitionemque et decisionem illarum nobis reservamus." —*Fontes,* n. 90.

[84] *Commentaria, ibid.,* n. 169.

[85] Canon 1770, § 1.

[86] D. XXII (5, 3), 3; *Novellae,* 90, 5.

receiving the citation to appear they must inform the court of the place they have selected.[87]

In concluding this treatment of the privileges enjoyed by cardinals relative to judicial procedure, it should be pointed out that although cardinals enjoy in their titles and deaconries most of the rights that a bishop enjoys in his diocese, they may not concern themselves with any judicial matters that pertain to their titles or deaconries.[88] From the year 1692 in the pontificate of Innocent XII all judicial matters concerning the titles and deaconries of Rome have been placed in the hands of the Cardinal Vicar of the City.

Article II. Cardinalitial Exemption from General Penal Legislation

Canon 2227, § 1. Poena nonnisi a Romano Pontifice infligi aut declarari potest in eos de quibus in canon 1557, § 1.

§ 2. Nisi expresse nominentur, S.R.E. Cardinales sub lege poenali non comprehenduntur, nec Episcopi sub poenis latae sententiae suspensionis et interdicti.

The Code in treating of persons who are subject to the penal legislation of the Church exempts cardinals from every penal law in which they are not expressly named. When one considers that the whole of Book V of the Code is devoted to penal matters, one can appreciate the vast extension of this privilege.

Historically this privilege has been enjoyed in a lesser degree by the cardinals for centuries. Because of its all-inclusive extension as enunciated in the Code, it must be considered as new with the Code.

[87] Canon 1770, § 2, n. 1: Testes sunt examini subiiciendi in ipsa tribunalis sede. Ab hac generali regula excipiuntur: S.R.E. Cardinales Episcopi et personae illustres quae suae civitatis iure eximuntur ab obligatione comparendi coram iudice testificandi causa: ii omnes eligere ipsi possunt locum ubi testificentur, de quo iudicem certiorem facere debent.

[88] Canon 240, § 2: Ceteri Cardinales in suis titulis vel diaconiis, postquam eorundem canonicam possessionem ceperint, omnia possunt quae locorum Ordinarii in suis ecclesiis, exceptis ordine iudiciorum et qualibet iurisdictione in fideles. . . .

Innocent IV (1243-1254) in the First General Council of Lyons (1245) decreed that bishops *and other superior prelates* were not to be considered as included in any penal enactment that stipulated *ipso facto* punishments of interdict or suspension, unless such persons are expressly mentioned.[39] Excommunication, according to Lega, was not included in this privilege as it was a punishment inflicted only on crimes so enormous that not even the dignity of bishops or other superior prelates was sufficient to warrant their exemption.[40]

It was the common opinion of pre-Code authors that cardinals enjoyed this privilege granted by Innocent IV in virtue of the phrase *"alii superiores praelati"* which comprehended cardinals. Consequently, cardinals unless expressly mentioned were not subject to *ipso facto* punishments of interdict or suspension, but were subject to penalties that involved excommunication since this decree did not exempt them from excommunications unless expressly mentioned.[41]

The concept of a cardinalitial exemption from all penal laws which do not expressly mention cardinals began to flourish chiefly among commentators of the *Regulae Cancellariae,* which first appeared in written form during the pontificate of John XXII (1316-1334).[42] From the time of John XXII it was the custom for each

[39] C. 4, *de sententia excommunicationis,* V, 11, in VI°: "Quia periculosum est episcopis et eorum superioribus propter exsecutionem pontificalis officio, quod frequenter incumbit, ut in aliquo casu interdicti vel suspensionis incurrant sententiam ipso facto, nos deliberatione provida duximus statuendum, ut episcopi et alii superiores praelati nullius constitutionis occasione, sententiae sive mandati, praedictam incurrant sententiam ullatenus ipso iure, nisi in ipsis de episcopis expressa mentio habeatur."

[40] Cf. Lega, *Praelectiones in Textum Iuris Canonici, De Delictis et Poenis* (2. ed., Romae, 1910), n. 117.

[41] Bishops today continue to enjoy this restricted exemption. They are still subject to penalties involving excommunication even if they are not expressly mentioned (canon 2227, § 2).

[42] As the exercise of ecclesiastical power became more and more centralized, the work that fell to the hands of the Roman Pontiff became increasingly involved. To facilitate the speedy transaction of this growing business the Popes issued a set of practical regulations as a guide for the Roman Curia. At first these rules were in the form of oral instructions. It remained for John XXII to reduce them to writing and thus supply the initial movement which

pontiff on the day following his election to confirm and promulgate the Chancery Rules of his predecessor, introducing whatever changes he desired to make. From the pontificate of Clement XI (1700-1721) no further changes or additions were made to the *Regulae Cancellariae*.[43]

Regula LXX of the Chancery Rules promulgated by Clement XII (1730-1740),[44] is the following:

> *"Cum S.R.E. Cardinales sanctissimo domino nostro assistant, ac propterea debeant specialibus praerogativis et privilegiis gaudere, idem dominus noster statuit, ordinavit et declaravit quod in quibuscumque constitutionibus et regulis per Sanctitatem Suam edendis non comprehendantur neque comprehensi censeantur ipsi Cardinales, nisi illae eorundem Cardinalium favorem concernant, vel constitutiones edendae de eorumdem Cardinalium vel maioris partis eorum consilio editae fuerint, seu in eisdem regulis et constitutionibus facta fuerit ipsorum Cardinalium expressa mentio."* [45]

This rule was first added to the *Regulae Cancellariae* by Leo X (1513-1521) and was subsequently confirmed and promulgated by his successors.

The rule stated that cardinals were not to be considered comprehended in any future rules or apostolic constitutions that concern

was to determine their form under the succeeding pontiffs. The first group of *Regulae Cancellariae* had to do with the expedition of *litterae gratiae et justitiae* from the Apostolic Chancery. A second class known as judicial rules was drawn up and added by Nicholas V (1447-1455). A third class added by various popes until the time of Clement XI (1700-1721) dealt with *reservationes* and had special reference to reserved benefices. Cf. Ottenthal, *Regulae Cancellariae Apostolicae, Die Päpstlichen Kanzleiregeln von Johannes XXII bis Nicolaus V* (Innsbruck, 1888), p. ix; Haydt, *Reserved Benefices,* The Catholic University of America Canon Law Studies, n. 161 (Washington, D. C.: The Catholic University of America Press, 1942), pp. 31 ff.

[43] Cf. Van Hove, *Prolegomena Ad Codicem Iuris Canonici (Commentarium Lovaniense,* Vol. I, tom. I, Mechliniae et Romae: Dessain, 1928), p. 190.

[44] As the rules promulgated by Clement XII are identical with those of Clement XI, quotations will be taken from those of Clement XII since these rules are more readily accessible to the writer. These rules of Clement XII may be found in *Bull. Rom.,* XXIII, 18 ff.

[45] *Bull. Rom.,* XXIII, 18.

materia odiosa, unless the constitutions or rules were edited upon the advice of at least the majority of cardinals, or unless express mention of the cardinals is made therein.

This rule gave rise to two schools of thought among the commentators. Riganti [46] and Gomez,[47] among others, held that in virtue of Regula LXX cardinals, unless expressly mentioned, were exempt *only* from future chancery rules that might be made. Riganti [48] phrased his opinion as follows:

> *"Dum Regula LXX eximit tantummodo Cardinales a Cancellariae Regulis in posterum edendis, si eorum expressa mentio facta non fuerit, nequit illius dispositio, concurrente etiam identitate reationis, protendi ad exemptionem a caeteris dispositionibus et ordinationibus Apostolicis, quibus ipsi de iure communi subiecti sunt, si odiosa non sint odio irrationabili, materiam contineant ipsis quoque Cardinalibus proportionatam, et sint conceptae verbis aptis illos comprehendere."*

It should be noted that even Riganti, as appears from the excerpt quoted above, and Gomez,[49] conceded that if the matter concerned is *odiosa* and cardinals are not expressly mentioned, they may be considered as not comprehended in the enactment. Since *poenae* are certainly classified as *res odiosae,*[50] it may be concluded that when not expressly mentioned cardinals were not considered as comprehended in penal enactments.[51]

The second school of commentators basing their opinion on the very general wording of Regula LXX expressly concluded that the Popes intended to exempt cardinals from all future constitutions and dispositions (*"quibuscumque constitutionibus"*) that concerned *materia odiosa,* unless express mention was made that cardinals were

[46] *Commentaria,* tom. IV, in Reg. LXX, n. 44.

[47] *Commentaria in Regulas Cancellariae Iudiciales* (Lugduni, 1543), Proemium and p. 153.

[48] *Loco citato.*

[49] *Op. cit.,* p. 153.

[50] Cf. canon 19; Reg. 15, R.J., in VI°.

[51] Cf. Albanus, *De Cardinalatu,* quest. XLII, pp. XCII-XCV; Germonius, *De Sacrorum Immunitatibus,* p. 166, n. 55.

subject to such enactments. This seems to have been the more common opinion as Cardinal Tuscus noted.[52]

Even prior to the appearance of this chancery rule, the opinion that cardinals unless expressly mentioned were exempt from penal enactments had been put forth by Ioannes Monachus (+ 1313), Ioannes Andreae (1272-1348) and Panormitanus (Nicolaus de Tudeschis) (1386-1453). These commentators on the decretals based their opinion on a penal decretal of Boniface VIII,[53] wherein Boniface in order to subject cardinals to the punishments enunciated in the decree expressly mentioned them.

Cardinal Tuscus formulated the opinion of the second school of thought thusly:

> *"Sub generali dispositione odiosa, sicuti Senatores non comprehenduntur sed Imperatori reservantur; ita etiam Cardinales in generali dispositione odiosa Papae non includuntur quia speciali nota digni sunt. Constitutiones poenales non comprehendunt Cardinales, nisi in specie exprimantur."* [54]

The general argument of this school was this: cardinals unless expressly mentioned are not subject to decrees that involve *materia odiosa;* but, poenal matters are *materiae odiosae.* Therefore, cardinals are not subject to penal enactments unless expressly mentioned.

Diana (1586-1663) expressed the opinion as follows:

> *"Cardinales non tenentur in quavis dispositione poenali, nisi de eis fiat expressa mentio."* [55]

Though this latter opinion was the more common, prior to the promulgation of the Code it was never accorded full legal force. It was canonized by the Code in canon 2227, § 2 and therefore now has full legal force so that cardinals are not subject to any penal decree in which they are not expressly mentioned.

[52] *Conclusiones Frequentiores,* I, C, concl. 100, n. 27.

[53] C. un., *de schismaticis,* V, 3, in VI°. Published in the year 1297—Potthast, n. 24520.

[54] *Ibid.,* nn. 26, 29.

[55] *Resolutiones Morales,* V, tom. IX, tract. 7, res. XXXI; cf. Cohellius, *Notitia Cardinalatus* (Romae, 1653), p. 172.

In virtue of the present law, cardinals are exempt from all censures including those of excommunication, whether *latae* or *ferendae sententiae* in which they are not expressly mentioned. The Code contains only two such penal laws in which cardinals are expressly mentioned. These are found in canons 2332 and 2397.[56]

Besides those contained in the Code as such, the Constitution *Vacante Sede Apostolica* (Pius X, December 25, 1904) contained in the appendix of the Code mentions various *ipso facto* excommunications for delicts committed in papal elections and the Constitution *Commissum nobis* (Pius X, January 20, 1904) also contained in the appendix of the Code mentions another censure connected with papal elections.

Papal elections are now exclusively ruled by the Constitution of Pius X, *Vacante Sede Apostolica.*[57] The cardinals, as a body, have the exclusive privilege of electing the Sovereign Pontiff. The historical evolution of this cardinalitial privilege was the following.

In the year 1059 with the legislation of Pope Nicholas II (1059-1061), cardinals became the principal electors of the Supreme Pontiff.[58] With the decree *Licet de vitanda of* Alexander III (1159-1181), promulgated in the Third Lateran Council (1179),[59] cardinals were constituted the exclusive electors of the Pope. A two-third majority vote was required that the election be canonical. Gregory X (1271-1276) in his *Ubi periculum*[60] instituted the conclave and enacted legislation whose intent it was to accelerate the proceedings therein. Clement V (1305-1314) with a like intention of accelerating the conclave proceedings, allowed cardinals under ex-

[56] Canon 2332: Omnes et singuli cuiusque status, gradus seu conditionis etiam regalis, episcopalis vel cardinalitiae fuerint, a legibus, decretis, mandatis Romani Pontificis pro tempore existentis ad Universale Concilium appellantes, sunt suspecti de haeresi et ipso facto contrahunt excommunicationem Sedi Apostolicae speciali modo reservatam; . . .

Canon 2397: Si quis ad dignitatem cardinalitium promotus, iusiurandum, de quo in can. 234, emittere recusaverit, ipso facto cardinalitia dignitate privatus perpetuo maneat.

[57] Canon 160.

[58] C. 1, D. XXIII.

[59] C. 6, X, *de electione et electi potestate,* I, 6.

[60] C. 3, *de electione et electi potestate,* I, 6, in VI°.

communication, suspension or interdict the right of entering the conclave and voting.[61] Julius II (1503-1513) legislated against simony, covering the various aspects under which it might creep into the election of the Vicar of Christ on earth.[62] Pius IV (1559-1565) with his constitution *In eligendis* inaugurated the *"congregatio particularis"* which was to consist of three cardinals, one from each rank, who together with the Camerlengo were to take charge of minor affairs of the Church during the conclave. At the end of three days the next three cardinals in seniority would constitute this congregation, etc.[63] Gregory XV (1621-1623) allowed the cardinals to follow any one of three forms of election: *scrutinium, compromissum* or *quasi-inspiratio.* He decreed that no cardinal could vote for himself and enacted provisions for computing the ballots which were to be burned immediately afterward. No other major enactments were promulgated until the time of Pius X (1903-1914) who abrogated all preceding legislation, excepting only the Constitution *Predecessores nostri* of Leo XIII (1878-1903), and his own previous constitution, *Commissum Nobis* (20 ian. 1904), with his constitution *Vacante Sede Apostolica* of December 25, 1904. With his Constitution *Commissum Nobis* of January 20, 1904, he had forbidden under pain of excommunication any cardinal or other person to make use of the so-called civil *veto* or *exclusiva,* by which civil powers formerly had made known their objections against certain candidates. Pius XI changed several provisions of the *Vacante Sede Apostolica* by his Motu proprio, *Cum proxime,* of March 1, 1922, which also is appended to the Code. The chief amendment of Pius XI was to extend the time allowed by Pius X between the death of the Pope and the opening of the conclave from ten to fifteen days. He gave the cardinals the power of further extending the interval to a maximum of eighteen days.

With regard to the delicts that might be committed in the process of electing a new Pope and their punishments, the Code rules that they are governed exclusively by the *Vacante Sede Apostolica*

[61] C. 2, *de electione et electi potestate,* I, 3 in Clem.

[62] *Bull. Rom.,* V, 405.

[63] *Bull. Rom.,* VII, 230.

of Pius X.[64] In that constitution there are eight cases in which excommunication *ipso facto* may be incurred [65] and in the Constitution *Commissum Nobis* there is another, making nine in all. These are reserved for absolution to the Holy Father himself, and absolution cannot be given by any other, not even the Cardinal Major Penitentiary, except in danger of death.[66]

In all of these penal enactments with the single exception of the *latae sententiae* excommunication sanctioning all simony and simoniacal transactions of any kind,[67] cardinals are expressly mentioned. Therefore, there can be no doubt that they are subject to these censures and should incur them *ipso facto* were they guilty of the delicts to which the excommunications are attached.

The censure punishing a delict of simony in a papal election raises a perplexing problem. Cardinals are not expressly mentioned in it and as a consequence, the question arises: Did the legislator intend to subject cardinals to it? As worded in the constitution, the enactment is as follows:

> *"Simoniae crimen, tam divino quam humano iure detestabile, in electione Romani Pontificis omnino sicut reprobatum esse constat, ita et Nos reprobamus atque damnamus, huiusque criminis reos poena excommunicationis latae sententiae innodamus; sublata tamen irritatione electionis simoniacae, quam Deus avertat, a Iulio II (vel alio qualicumque decreto pontificio) statuta, ut praetextus amputetur impugnandi valorem electionis Romani Pontificis."* [68]

On the one hand, since cardinals are not expressly mentioned in this penalty, as they are in the other seven censures contained in this constitution, it would seem that they are not subject to the excommunication. In virtue of canon 2330 [69] it is asserted that this

[64] Canon 2330: Quod attinet ad poenas statutas in delicta quae in eligendo Summo Pontifice committi possunt, unice standum const. Pii X *Vacante Sede Apostolica*, 25 Dec. 1904.

[65] Nn. 37, 51, 52, 69, 79, 80, 81 and 82.

[66] Const., *Vacante Sede Apostolica*, tit. 2, cap. 4, n. 51.

[67] N. 79.

[68] Const. *Vacante Sede Apostolica*, n. 79.

[69] Cf. *above*, footnote 64.

constitution is implicitly a part of the Code as the word *"unice"* used in canon 2330 merely means that the penalties are to be drawn from this constitution of Pius X to the exclusion of other constitution on the same matter. This is an argument used by Blat.[70] In view of this statement, canon 2227, § 2 seems to be applicable to the penalties of the *Vacante Sede Apostolica,* and since cardinals are not expressly mentioned in the penalty for simony, they can be considered as exempted from it. For, in accordance with canon 19,[71] those laws which inflict a penalty must be strictly interpreted, and in case of doubt, the more lenient interpretation is to be followed.[72] Such is the argument that would exempt cardinals from incurring this penalty.

On the other hand, despite the fact that cardinals are not expressly mentioned, the peculiar nature of this constitution would seem to demand that cardinals be comprehended in the phrase *"huiusque criminis reos."* The constitution deals with papal elections in which cardinals are at one and the same time the exclusive electors, and, practically speaking, the most probable candidates. Therefore, from the end and object of the constitution, it seems to the writer that whatever is said in it concerns primarily cardinals, in whose hands have been placed the various agenda of the papal election.

Moreover, simony of its very nature implies complicity.[73] This being true, in papal elections one party to the simoniacal agreement would almost of necessity be a cardinal, since they alone elect the new pontiff. For, as Ryder notes,[74] "the penalty established by the Constitution (*Vacante Sede Apostolica*) is restricted to simony concerning the election itself, and cannot be said to pertain to other secondary matters e. g. the choosing of the officials of the conclave, nor to any mercenary attempts to win the favor of the cardinal-

[70] *Commentarium,* V, n. 171.

[71] Canon 19: Leges quae poenam statuunt, aut liberum iurium exercitium coarctant, aut exceptionem a lege continent, strictae subsunt interpretationi.

[72] Canon 2219, § 1: In poenis benignior est interpretatio facienda.

[73] Ryder, *Simony,* The Catholic University of America Canon Law Studies, n. 65 (Washington, D. C.: The Catholic University of America, 1931), p. 72.

[74] *Op. cit.,* p. 132.

electors unless the latter might be equivalent to the purchase of votes. In other words, simony in papal elections consists in any onerous contract in which the Cardinals' votes are bought and sold, or by which an obligation of temporal compensation is placed in exchange for the election. Stipulations for the increase of the Cardinals' *honorarium*, or obligations to confer upon them offices, benefices or dignities in return for their votes, would also fall within the scope of censure. The excommunication would also be incurred if the promise of a vote were made to a friend or relative of the nominee on condition that he would use his influence with the new Pope to secure some recompense for the elector."

Another argument supporting the contention that cardinals are subject to this censure is that the Constitution of Julius II (1503-1513), *Cum tam divino* [75] upon which this section of Pius X's Constitution is based, expressly mentioned cardinals as the subjects of the penalty for simony.

To the writer, the fact that cardinals are not expressly mentioned in this enactment is of little consequence, for with Vermeersch-Creusen [76] the writer maintains that canon 2227, § 2 cannot be applied to this constitution of Pius X. Canon 160 [77] expressly states that papal elections are governed *exclusively* (*"unice"*) by the Constitution *Vacante Sede Apostolica.* Therefore, as the canon notes, such elections are not subject to the general laws that govern elections in the Code. Similarly, canon 2330 [78] states that punishments for crimes perpetrated in papal elections are governed exclusively

[75] 14 ian. 1505—*Bull Rom.*, V, 405. It is to be noted that in the Constitution of Julius II not only were the guilty parties censured but the election itself when tainted by simony was null and void. In order that the accusation of simony might not continue to furnish men with a pretext for attacking the validity of papal elections, Pius X saw fit to remove the invalidating clause from the law governing the election of the Supreme Pontiff.

[76] *Epitome*, III, n. 530, 5.

[77] Canon 160: Romani Pontificis electio unice regitur const. Pii X *Vacante Sede Apostolica*, 25 Dec. 1904; in aliis electionibus ecclesiasticis serventur praescripta canonum qui sequuntur, et peculiaria, si qua sint, pro singulis officiis legitime statuta.

[78] Cf. *above*, p. 126, footnote 64.

(*"unice"*) by the statutes of Pius X's Constitution.[79] Therefore, it may be legitimately concluded that the stipulation of canon 2227, § 2 is not applicable to this Constitution.

Ryder,[80] because of the delicate nature of this question and the diversity of opinion concerning it, was content to repeat the words of Cappello: [81] *"Nostram sententiam proferre non audemus. Videant sapientiores."* The writer, not presuming to constitute himself a *"sapientior,"* nevertheless, in view of the foregoing arguments, is of the opinion (*salva reverentia et meliori iudicio*) that cardinals are subject to this censure by which simoniacal transactions in papal elections are punished, and that they are to be considered as comprehended in the generic words used by Pius X, *"huiusque criminis reos."*

In concluding this chapter, mention must be made of a final cardinalitial privilege in these matters. It is this: should a cardinal have incurred the censure of a penal canon to which he is expressly subject, the declaration of a sentence in that regard is reserved to the exclusive competence of the Roman Pontiff. No one else may issue such a declaratory sentence.[82]

[79] The writer maintains with Vermeersch-Creusen (*Epitome,* III, n. 530, 5) that the more correct interpretation of this word *"unice"* is *"exclusively,"* i.e., to the exclusion of all other penal laws.

[80] *Op. cit.,* p. 134.

[81] *De Censuris,* n. 571.

[82] Cf. canon 2227, § 1, as quoted at the beginning of this article.

CHAPTER X

MISCELLANEOUS PRIVILEGES

Article I. Privilege of Attending General Councils With the Right to a Decisive Vote

Canon 223, § 1, n. 1. Vocantur ad Concilium (Oecumenicum) in eoque habent ius suffragii deliberativi: S.R.E. Cardinales, etsi non epsicopi.

All cardinals are *privileged* to be present at General Councils of the Church with the right of a decisive vote in all matters voted on by such a Council. This privilege like the others contained in the Code, directly refers to cardinals as such. If a cardinal is also a patriarch, a primate, a residential archbishop or bishop, then in virtue of the fact that he is a local Ordinary, he would necessarily have a right to attend.

This cardinalitial privilege is based on the dignity and precedence that all cardinals, even thought not bishops, enjoy over all other ecclesiastics of the Church inferior to the Supreme Pontiff. The privilege in question seems to have been definitely conceded during the pontificate of Pope Eugene IV (1431-1447), who by his Constitution *Non mediocri* (a. 1439) definitely established the cardinalitial prerogative of out-ranking, after the Pope himself, all other ecclesiastics. The privilege as such, however, does not seem to have been enunciated until after the pontificate of Eugene IV.

Cardinal Bellarmine (1542-1621) expressly referred to the right of cardinals to be present at General Councils and to have a decisive vote as a privilege that was customarily accorded them even though they were not bishops.[1] Though Bellarmine attributed the cardi-

[1] *De Controversiis Christianae Fidei adversus huius temporis Haereticos* (3 vols. in 2, ed. cura Card. Sforza, Neapoli, 1856-1858) II, Lib. I: *De Conciliis et Ecclesia,* C. XV: "Catholicorum sententia est solos praelatos maiores

nals' presence at general councils with decisive vote to a privilege they enjoyed by custom, Suarez (1548-1617) asserted that it was more probable that all cardinals had a right to be present and to cast deciding votes "*ex iure ordinario.*" This was evident, he claimed, from the fact that cardinals *affixed* their signatures before those of bishops at the Fifth Lateran Council (1512-1517).[2]

Diana (1586-1663) expressly emphasized this cardinalitial prerogative, indicating that Cardinals were to precede bishops at these Councils.[3]

In more recent times previous to the Code this cardinalitial prerogative was evidenced in the fact that Pius IX (1846-1878) in establishing the precedence to be accorded the various Fathers of the Vatican Council listed the Fathers in the respective order that is now found in canon 223, § 1 of the Code, cardinals being first.[4]

That this prerogative of all cardinals, even of those who are not bishops, partakes of the full nature of a privilege is evidenced from the fact that all the other ecclesiastics enumerated in canon 223, § 1 [5] are *Ordinarii* with proper jurisdiction in the external forum, who,

eosque omnes, idest Episcopos, in conciliis generalibus et provincialibus habere ius suffragii decisivi ordinarie, *ex privilegio autem et consuetudine, etiam cardinales . . . licet episcopi non sint.* (Italics are the writer's.)

[2] *Opera Omnia* (26 vols., Parisiis, 1856-1861), XII, tract. I, disput. VI: *De Conciliis*, p. 327, n. 17: "Probabilius est Cardinales nunc ex iure ordinario pertinere ad generale concilium sive id habeant a iure divino, sive Pontificio; quod etiam penda ex illa quaestione, an Cardinalium dignitas sit iure humano introducta, ut vult Scotus, vel divino ut tenet Turrecremata et alii; quidquid vero de hoc sit, iam Doctores omnes conveniunt Cardinales habere suffragium definitivum in Concilio. . . . Ratio est, quia iam ex usu et concessione Pontificum, praeferuntur Cardinales Episcopis in his quae episcopalis consecratio essentialiter non fundat; tun etiam quia in suis titulis habent iurisdictionem episcopalem. Unde in Concilio Lateranensi sub Leone X (Fifth General Council of the Lateran, 1512-1517), ante Episcopos subscribunt Cardinales. . . ."

[3] *Resolutiones Morales*, V, Tom. 9, tract. 7, res. XVII: "Cardinales qui episcopi non sunt, non solum votem habent decisivam ut Episcopi, sed praeferuntur Episcopis ut videri potest apud Concilium Lateranense, ibi enim ante Episcopis scripserunt Cardinales."

[4] Litt. ap. "*Multiplices,*" 27 nov. 1869, n. IV—*Fontes*, n. 553.

[5] Patriarchs, Primates, Archbishops, Residential Bishops including those not yet consecrated, Abbots or Prelates *nullius*, Prime Abbots, Abbot-Superiors

therefore, have a definite right to be present with the right to a deciding vote, since matters to be discussed and decided in general councils are primarily jurisdictional matters.[6] Cardinals as such are not Ordinaries, hence their privilege.

Any cardinal who is legitimately impeded from attending must send a proxy to explain his absence. If one having a right to assist at the council is selected by the cardinal as his proxy, he enjoys only one vote. Should the cardinal's proxy be an ecclesiastic who ordinarily would have no right to attend, this proxy automatically acquires the right of being present, but only for the public sessions. However, such a proxy enjoys neither a consultive or deliberative vote although he is permitted to affix his signature, as the cardinal's proxy, to the completed acts of the council.[7]

Finally, a cardinal, or his proxy if he himself has been legitimately impeded from attending, may not leave the Council before its completion, unless the presiding officer of the Council shall have approved the reason given and have granted the necessary permission to leave.[8]

Article II. Privilege of Exemption From the Ecclesiastical Prohibition of Books

Canon 1401. S.R.E. Cardinales, Episcopi etiam titulares, aliique Ordinarii, necessariis adhibitis cautelis, ecclesiastica librorum prohibitione non adstringuntur.

It is explicitly stated in the Code that cardinals are not bound by the ecclesiastical prohibition of books, provided that in reading

of Monastic Congregations and the Supreme Moderators of Clerical Exempt Religious.

[6] Cf. Beste, *Introductio in Codicem,* p. 232.

[7] Canon 224. For a more complete treatment on the rights of proxies at Ecumenical Councils, the reader is referred to Connors, *Extra-Judicial Procurators in the Code of Canon Law,* The Catholic University of America Canon Law Studies, n. 192 (Washington, D. C.: The Catholic University of America Press, 1944), pp. 51-55.

[8] Canon 225: Nemini eorum qui Concilio interesse debent, licet ante discedere, quam Concilium sit rite absolutum, nisi a Concilii praeside cognita ac probata discessionis causa et impetrata abeundi licentia.

such books they employ the necessary precautions. Now the ecclesiastical prohibition of consists in this: all books that are forbidden in accordance with the norms of canon 1399 may not without due permission be published, read, retained, sold or translated into another language, or communicated to others in any manner.[9] This prohibition is sanctioned by an *ipso facto* excommunication reserved for absolution to the Holy See *speciali modo*.[10] Cardinals, then, in virtue of this exemption may without seeking any permission, read and keep in their possession the various types of books that treat of matters mentioned in canon 1399 as well as those books specifically mentioned in the *Index of Prohibited Books* and in all special decrees of the Holy See, provided the cardinals in doing so employ the necessary precautions. Because third parties are necessarily involved when such books are sold, translated or communicated to others, the cardinalitial exemption does not extend to the laws of previous censorship, but is restricted to the reading and possession of such books in accordance with canon 1403, § 2.[11]

Historically, it was always understood in the Church that the prohibition of books did not bind equally the people and the hierarchy. The reason was that the hierarchy must be on the lookout for pernicious literature to be able to warn the people against it and, whenever necessary, to refute error. Besides, the knowledge of religion and the piety required for such a high office makes them less vulnerable to these insidious snares than others.[12] Only in exceedingly difficult times did the Church extend her prohibition to the members of the hierarchy, e. g. in her condemnation of Iconoclast literature at the Second Nicene Council (787),[13] and in her pro-

9 Canon 1398.

10 Canon 2318.

11 Canon 1403, § 2: Qui facultatem apostolicam consecuti sunt legendi et retinendi libros prohibitos . . . gravi praecepto tenentur libros prohibitos ita custodiendi, ut hi ad aliorum manus non perveniant. Cf. Augustine, *Commentary*, VI, 477.

12 Cf. Pernicone, *The Ecclesiastical Prohibition of Books*, The Catholic University of America Canon Law Studies, n. 72 (Washington, D. C.: The Catholic University of America, 1932), 196.

13 Mansi, XIII, 429.

scription of Luther's writings in 1520.[14] From the time of Luther and the Protestant Reformation to the present Code, bishops and other members of the hierarchy were obliged to secure permission from the Holy See to read books forbidden by the positive law of the Church.

That cardinals prior to the Code were obliged to secure this permission is evidenced from the following historical documents.

Pius IV (1559-1565) in publishing his Index and its accompanying rules allowed no exceptions to his prohibition. He declared:

> *"Inhibentes omnibus et singulis tam ecclesiasticis personis saecularibus, et regularibus cuiuscumque gradus, ordinis et dignitatis sint, quam laicis . . . ne quis contra earum regularum praescriptum, aut ipsius prohibitionem Indicis libros ullos legere, hebereve audeat. . . ."* [15]

The same pontiff a few months later appointed a group of cardinal-inquisitors to inspect books of dubious doctrine, and lest they might suffer from any scruples in performing these duties, the Pope expressly conceded them special faculties to read and retain heretical books, in these words:

> *"Ad omnem haesitandi materiam et conscientiae scrupulum in eis tollendum, motu simili et ex certa nostra scientia . . . de eorundem . . . cardinalium fide, probitate et constantia singularem tum notitiam, tum fiduciam habentes, eisdem cardinalibus concedimus, ut durante eorum officio et quamdiu inquisitioni huiusmodi praefuerint, quoscumque, quaecumque, quotcumque et qualiacumque quorumcumque . . . infidelium et haereticorum . . . commentaria, tractatus, libros, collectanea . . . habere, tenere, legere absque aliquo conscientiae scrupulo . . . libere et licite possint et valeant. . . ."* [16]

From this it can be concluded that from the time of the Protestant Reformation not even cardinals were permitted to read or retain

[14] Leo X, const. *"Exsurge Domine,"* 15 iun. 1520—*Fontes,* n. 76.

[15] Const. *"Dominici gregis,"* 24 martii 1564, § 3—*Fontes,* n. 105. For a complete historical treatment of the ecclesiastical prohibition of books, the reader may consult Pernicone, *op. cit.,* 11-67.

[16] *"Cum inter crimina,"* 27 aug. 1564, § 2—*Bull. Rom.,* VII, 301.

any forbidden book without first having obtained the necessary permission. But, since the promulgation of the Code, all cardinals from the moment of their consistorial appointment receive the faculty to read and retain any forbidden book provided they observe the necessary precautions.

Canon 1401 uses the phrase *"necessariis adhibitis cautelis,"* but does not determine these precautions. They may be described as follows:

(a) The natural as well as the positive law requires that no one should expose his faith and morals unnecessarily to danger (canon 1405, § 1), for no one is immune from temptations.

(b) No one is allowed to read lascivious or obscene books unless he is bound *ex officio* to examine them.

(c) If a cardinal retains in his possession a forbidden book, he must see to it that the book does not fall into the hands of those not permitted to read such a book.[17]

These necessary precautions may be summed up as anything that the natural law urges upon an individual cardinal as necessary to remove any spiritual danger to himself as well as any occasion of scandal for others.[18]

Finally in this matter, it is to be noted that the exemption is personal to cardinals as such, based on the high moral and spiritual qualities of an ecclesiastic who is raised to the cardinalate. Consequently, the permission contained in canon 1401 cannot be delegated to others by a cardinal. Of course, if a cardinal is also a residential bishop, he is empowered by the common law to grant permission to his subjects to read certain specific books in urgent cases.[19]

Article III. Privilege of Entering the Cloister in Religious Houses of Nuns and Sisters

Canon 600, n. 3. Intra monialium clausuram nemo, cuiusvis generis, conditionis, sexus, aetatis admittatur

[17] Cf. Augustine, *Commentary,* VI, 477.

[18] Cf. Blat, *Commentarium,* III, n. 290.

[19] Canon 1406, § 1. Cf. Pernicone, *op. cit.,* p. 200.

sine Sanctae Sedis licentia, exceptis personis quae sequuntur: . . . itemque S.R.E. Cardinales.

Canon 604, § 1. In domibus etiam Congregationum religiosarum sive pontificii sive dioecesani iuris clausura servetur, in quam nemo alterius sexus admittatur, nisi ii de quibus in canon 598, § 2 et canon 600, aliique quos ex iustis et rationabilibus causis Superiores admitti posse censuerint.

Another privilege extended by the Code to all Cardinals because of their eminent dignity is that of entering into the cloister in the religious houses both of nuns and sisters.[20]

Section 1. The Cloister of Nuns

The cloister observed by nuns is the *papal* cloister, i. e., it is governed in all its details, including the penalties for its violation, by the General law of the Church, and is obligatory on nuns properly so called, i. e., those female religious who take solemn vows. Members of a religious order that normally take solemn vows, but owing to circumstances are allowed to take only simple vows are still called *nuns*.[21]

Canon 600 denies admission into the papal cloister of nuns to all persons, regardless of their social condition, sex or age, unless such persons have first received the permission of the Holy See. This

[20] Canons 600, n. 3; 604, § 1; 488, n. 7: . . . ; *sororum* (Sisters), religiosae votorum simplicium; *monialium* (nuns), religiosae votorum sollemnium aut, nisi ex rei natura vel ex contextu sermonis aliud constet, religiosae quarum vota ex instituto sunt sollemnia, sed pro aliquibus locis ex Apostolicae Sedis praescripto sunt simplicia.

[21] Canon 488, n. 7. In the United States there are four convents of Visitation Nuns where solemn vows are taken and papal cloister is observed. These are situated in Georgetown (Washington, D. C.), Baltimore, St. Louis and Mobile. (Cf. S.C. Ep. et Reg., *Americana votorum,* 2 sept. 1865—*ASS,* I [1865], 708-739.) A fifth such convent situated at Kaskaskia, Illinois, and mentioned in the above decree has since been dissolved. All other nuns in this country take only simple vows and are bound only to the *episcopal* or modified cloister referred to in canon 604, § 1. Cf. Schaaf, *The Cloister,* The Catholic University of America Canon Law Studies, n. 13 (Washington, D. C.: The Catholic University of America, 1921), p. 104.

prohibition is sanctioned by an *ipso facto* excommunication reserved *simpliciter* to the Holy See.[22] A taxative list of persons excepted from this prohibition is included in canon 600, and among those listed are cardinals.

Since the reign of Boniface VIII (1294-1303), all persons have been excluded from the cloister of nuns unless there existed "a reasonable and manifest cause" for permitting such entry.[23] The Council of Trent permitted persons to be admitted "only in cases of necessity."[24]

The privilege accorded cardinals by the Code must be considered as entirely new. Gregory XIII (1572-1585) expressly forbade cardinals, among others, to enter the cloisters of nuns except in cases of real necessity.[25]

Diana (1586-1663), however, quoted the Rule of the Poor Clares which permitted cardinals to enter their cloisters even outside of a case of necessity.[26]

Although such an early edition of the Rule of the Poor Clares[27] was not available to the writer, it is possible that since Diana wrote shortly after the death of Gregory XIII,[28] the copy of the Rule he quoted from may have been an earlier one that did not contain the amendments required by Gregory's decree.

Regardless of the merits of Diana's opinion, it could no longer be sustained after the pontificate of Benedict XIV (1740-1758). This pontiff, confirming the decrees of his predecessors on the matter,

[22] Cf. canon 2342.

[23] C. un., *de statu regularium*, III, 16 in VI°.

[24] Sess. XXV, *de regularibus*, c. 5—Schroeder, *Canons and Decrees of the Council of Trent*, p. 221.

[25] Const. *"Dubiis,"* 23 dec. 1581, ad I—*Fontes*, n. 148.

[26] *Resolutiones Morales*, V, Tom. 9, tract. 7, res. XLIV. His quotation from the Rule of the Poor Clares was the following: *"Si quis de S.R.E. cardinalibus ad aliquod monasterium huiusmodi Religionis aliquando venire, et intra clausuram iugredi voluerit, cum reverentia quidem est suscipiendus; rogandus tamen ut cum paucis sociis ingrediatur."* This privilege, he noted, was not reserved to the cardinal-protector, but was extended to all cardinals.

[27] The order is officially known as the Franciscan Poor Clare Nuns, founded in Assisi, Italy, by Saint Clare in 1212.

[28] Diana was born (1586) the year following the death of Gregory XIII (1585).

expressly revoked all privileges that had been extended to any persons, *cardinals included,* permitting them to enter the cloisters of nuns.[29] This decree of Benedict XIV was in effect until the Code which has expressly permitted cardinals to enter any and all monasteries of nuns.

As Barry points out,[30] the concise wording of this cardinalitial privilege gave rise to much discussion among the authors, on the question of the lawfulness of a cardinal having his retinue accompany him when he enters such a cloister. In speaking of this privilege the canon (600, n. 3) does not explicitly include the phrase "*cum comitatu*" which is used in the first part of number 3 in referring to a similar privilege enjoyed by rulers and their wives.[31] However, the use of the word "*itemque*" seems sufficient to convey the meaning that cardinals are permitted, similarly as rulers and their wives, to take their retinue into the cloister with them.[32]

Blat occasioned the controversy by expressing in the first edition of his *Commentarium* the opinion that cardinals did not enjoy a right similar to that of rulers and their wives of taking their retinue with them when they enter a papal cloister of nuns.[33] Schaaf, following Blat, expressed the same opinion.[34] However, in the third edition of his *Commentarium,*[35] Blat has relinquished his former opinion and now holds the more common opinion that cardinals are permitted to have their retinues accompany them.

Section 2. The Episcopal or Modified Cloister of Sisters and Certain Nuns

Until the nineteenth century the Holy See recognized no cloister other than the papal one. In 1900, however, Leo XIII (1878-1903)

[29] Const. "*Salutare,*" 3 ian. 1742, n. 3—*Fontes,* n. 323.

[30] *Violation of the Cloister,* The Catholic University of America Canon Law Studies, n. 148 (Washington, D. C.: The Catholic University of America Press, 1942), p. 193.

[31] Cf. canon 600, n. 3, as quoted at beginning of this article.

[32] Cf. Vermeersch, "De Clausura Monialium,"—*Periodica,* XIX (1930), 12*-15*; Barry, *op. cit.,* p. 194.

[33] Cf. *Commentarium,* II (1921), n. 675.

[34] *The Cloister,* p. 123.

[35] II (3. ed., Romae: apud Angelicum, 1938), n. 533.

prescribed that in all congregations with papal approval, the episcopal or modified papal cloister was to be observed.[86] The Code now demands that a modified form of the papal cloister be observed in all congregations of religious women, whether of pontifical or only diocesan approval.[87] Consequently, *Sisters,* i. e., religious women who take only simple vows, as well as all *nuns* in the United States (except the four Visitation Convents at Georgetown, Baltimore, Mobile and St. Louis which are bound to observe papal cloister or others who may have a special Apostolic indult), are obliged to observe the modified form of the papal cloister known as the *episcopal* cloister. Regulations that govern the episcopal cloister are much more lenient than those governing papal cloisters. Whereas not even women are permitted to enter the papal cloister of nuns, entry into the cloister of sisters and nuns in the United States is forbidden only to men.[88]

Cardinals, however, in virtue of canon 604, § 1 are exempted from this prohibition and enjoy the same privilege regarding the episcopal cloister of sisters that they are granted for the papal cloister of nuns. This means that they are privileged to enter all cloisters of religious women and to take their retinues with them.

Article IV. Privilege of Preaching the Word of God Throughout the World

Canon 1337. Tum clericis e clero saeculari, tum religiosis non exemptis facultatem concionandi pro suo territorio solus concedit loci Ordinarius.

Canon 1338. Si concio habenda sit tantum ad religiosos exemptos aliosve de quibus in canon 514, § 1, facultatem concionandi in religione clericali dat eorum Superior secundum constitutiones.

Canon 239, § 1, n. 3. Cardinales facultate gaudent verbum Dei ubique praedicandi.

86 Const. *"Conditae a Nobis,"* 8 dec. 1900, ad II—*Fontes,* n. 644.

87 Canon 604, § 1.

88 Canon 604, § 1.

The general law of the Code stipulates that no one is permitted to exercise the ministry of preaching God's word unless he has received a commission from his legitimate superior either by special faculty or by appointment to an office to which the duty of preaching is attached by the Sacred Canons.[39] Permission to preach in any individual diocese must be obtained from the local Ordinary.[40] This also binds exempt religious when they are preaching to others than members of their institute.[41] For any priest to preach in a diocese other than the one to which he is incardinated, including all whether exempt or not when preaching to others than members of their institute, permission must first be obtained from the Ordinary of the place in which the sermon is to be delivered.[42]

All cardinals in virtue of the privilege conceded them by canon 239, § 1, n. 3 are exempted from this latter regulation of the common law and may preach the word of God in any diocese or exempt religious house throughout the world without the necessity of securing permission from anyone.[43] This faculty of cardinals is all-inclusive. No place or person is excepted from the extension of the faculty, not even nuns or clerical exempt religious. This privilege, which seems to be new with the Code, is another attestation of the exalted position of the cardinalate in the universal Church.

Article V. Privilege of Authenticating in the External Forum Any Verbal Privileges Granted by the Holy Father

Canon 79. Quamvis privilegia, oretenus a Sancta Sede obtenta, ipsi petenti in foro conscientiae suffragentur, nemo tamen potest cuiusvis privilegii usum adversus quemquam in foro externo vindicare, nisi

[39] Canon 1328.

[40] Canon 1337.

[41] Canon 1338, §§ 1 and 2.

[42] Canon 1341, § 1: Sacerdotes extradioecesani sive saeculares sive religiosi ad concionandum ne invitentur, nisi prius licentia ab Ordinario loci in quo concio habenda sit, obtenta fuerit; . . .

[43] Bishops also, in virtue of canon 349, enjoy this privilege, but they may only use it *"cum consensu saltem praesumpto Ordinarii loci."*

privilegium ipsum sibi concessum esse legitime evincat.

Canon 239, § 1, n. 17. Cardinales facultate gaudent fidem faciendi in foro externo, de oraculo pontificio testantes.

Oracula Pontificia or verbal privileges are those favors which have been granted orally to private persons by the Holy See. As privileges they have the same intrinsic value for the internal forum as written grants, for, that a privilege as such need not be written is evidenced from canon 79.[44] The Code declares that verbal privileges are of value in the internal forum at all times. Such oral privileges granted by the Holy See may also be used in the external forum even though their concession is not proved, *provided no one makes opposition thereto.* Such opposition would be had if the Ordinary requested the grantee of such a privilege to prove its concession, or when such a privilege demands the performance of a certain act on the part of another, or when it imposes a burden on some third party. Legal opposition would also be present should the grantee adduce such an oral privilege in an ecclesiastical trial.[45]

In all such cases, when the opposition is lawful, i. e. when the objection is raised by one who has a right to object, the grantee cannot use his privilege in the external forum unless he can furnish legal proof that he has received such a privilege from the Holy See.[46] That the necessity of such legal proof for oral privileges has long been the legislation of the Church is evidenced from the early decrees cited and quoted by Roelker.[47]

Legitimate proof may be established for such privileges in three ways: by witnesses, by prescription or by an authenticated document.[48] The presentation of an authenticated document is the most

[44] Cf. Reiffenstuel, *Ius Canonicum Universum* (6 vols., Romae, 1831-1834), Lib. V, Title XXXIII, n. 150; Roelker, *Principles of Privilege,* pp. 18, 38, 133; Cicognani, *Canon Law,* p. 826.

[45] Cf. Cicognani, *loc. cit.*

[46] Canon 79.

[47] *Op. cit.,* pp. 134-135.

[48] Roelker, *op. cit.,* pp. 136-137; Cicognani, *op. cit.,* p. 827.

satisfactory method for legally proving the concession of an oral privilege. For as Roelker points out, "possible suspicion of collusion in the case of witnesses, or possible bad faith unable to be detected in the case of prescription, hardly have any occasion to occur in the case of a document." [49]

It is precisely with such documents that the cardinalitial privilege conceded by canon 239, § 1, n. 17 is concerned. Any cardinal, in virtue of this privilege, can, from the time of his consistorial promotion, authenticate such a document testifying to a privilege that had been granted orally by the Holy Father (*"vivae vocis oraculo"*).

The privilege has reference to oracular pronouncements properly so called, i. e. concessions made to private persons by the Roman Pontiff or by the Roman Dicasteries or their officials, in favor of said private persons, or made to the cardinals and officials of the Roman Dicasteries themselves, but as private individuals. In such cases the testimony of a single cardinal is sufficient to constitute legal proof, whereas that of any other single person, even if he should be a dignitary, would not be sufficient.[50]

Accordingly, the testimony of the cardinal himself is sufficient proof of the fact that he himself had been the grantee of an oral privilege, and all similar privileges of other persons may be vindicated in the external forum when testified to by a cardinal.

This cardinalitial faculty, another that is directly based on their dignity in the Church, is referred to in canonical legislation as early as the pontificate of Pope Alexander III (1159-1181). In a decretal letter [51] this pontiff declared that a privilege of exemption that a certain monastery claimed to have been granted was still valid, despite the fact that the document had been lost. He based this judgment principally on the assertions of several cardinals who claimed to have seen the document in question. In commenting on this decree, the glossator pointed out that despite the fact that these

[49] *Op. cit.*, p. 136.

[50] Cf. Cicognani, *op. cit.*, p. 827, footnote (4).

[51] C. 12, X, *de privilegiis et excessibus privilegiatorum*, V, 33—Potthast, n. 720.

assertions were to be accepted, *"quia credit eis Papa tamquam fratribus suis et honestis viris."* [52]

Diana (1586-1663) [53] and Cardinal Tuscus,[54] among other pre-Code authors who mentioned this cardinalitial privilege, traced its origin to a decree of Pope Nicholas I (858-867),[55] in which the pontiff mentioned that he had accepted a certain legate solely because of the legate's dignity, despite the fact that he carried no letters of legation. From this the glossator concluded, *"ergo et Cardinali qui bene notus est in aliqua provincia, credendum esset sine litteris."* [56]

The legislator has incorporated the pre-Code privilege in the present Code and all cardinals now as formerly may authenticate documents testifying to a privilege that had been granted orally by the Holy Father, thus making the use of the privilege valid in the external forum.

Article VI. Privilege of Disposing of the Revenues of Their Benefices Either by Donation "Inter Vivos" or by Last Will

Canon 1473. Etsi beneficiarius alia bona non beneficialia habeat, libere uti frui potest fructibus beneficialibus qui ad eius honestam sustentationem sint necessarii; obligatione autem tenetur impendendi superfluos pro pauperibus aut piis causis, salvo praescripto canon 239, § 1, n. 19.

Canon 239, § 1, n. 19. Cardinales facultate gaudent de reditibus beneficiariis libere disponendi etiam per testamentum, salvo praescripto canon 1298.

Canon 1298, § 1. Defuncti S.R.E. Cardinalis, qui in Urbe domicilium habeat, quamvis Episcopus suburbicarius aut Abbas *nullius* esset, quaelibet sacra supellex,

[52] Gloss s. v. *"Fratribus"*; cf. Albanus, *De Cardinalatu*, ques. XLII, pp. LXXXIX-XC.

[53] *Resolutiones Morales*, V, Tom. 9, tract. 7, res. LXIX.

[54] *Conclusiones Frequentiores*, I, C, conclus. 103.

[55] C. 3, D. XCVII.

[56] Gloss s. v. *"nihilominus."*

> **exceptis annulis et crucibus pectoralibus etiam cum sacris reliquiis, aliaque res omnes stabiliter divino cultui destinatae, nulla habita ratione qualitatis et naturae redituum quibus comparatae sint, cedunt pontificio sacrario, nisi Cardinalis eas donaverit aut testamento reliquerit alicui ecclesiae vel oratorio publico vel loco pio vel alicui personae ecclesiasticae seu religiosae.**
>
> **Canon 1298, § 2. Optandum ut Cardinalis, qui huiusmodi facultate uti velit, saltem ex parte praeferat illas ecclesias, quas in titulum, administrationem seu commendam obtinuerit.**
>
> **Canon 1299, § 1. Defuncti Episcopi residentialis, etiamsi cardinalitia dignitate fulserit, sacra supellex cedit ecclesiae cathedrali, exceptis annulis et crucibus pectoralibus etiam cum sacris reliquiis, salvo praescripto canon 1288. . . .**

A cleric who is the incumbent of a benefice may freely make use of the revenues of his benefice that are necessary for his fitting sustenance, even though he may have revenues other than those coming from his benefice. He is, however, obliged to distribute whatever remains of the revenues of his benefice either to the poor or to a pious cause.[57] He is not permitted to dispose of the fruits of his benefice either by donations *inter vivos* or by last will.

The various goods that the incumbent of a benefice might have are the following: *bona patrimonalia,* i. e. his personal property that is in no way connected with the benefice; *bona quasi-patrimonalia* (*industrialia, casualia*), i. e. the funds that have come to a cleric

[57] Canon 1473. Whether this obligation is one based on commutative justice or one that flows from the virtue of religion (*ex obedientia*) has long been disputed. That it is only *ex obedientia* is the opinion of Vermeersch-Creusen, *Epitome,* II, 798; Vromant, *Ius Missionariorum,* Vol. VI, *De Bonis Temporalibus Ecclesiae* (Louvain, 1927), 216; De Meester, *Iuris Canonici et Iuris Canonico-Civilis Compendium* (4 vols., Brugis, 1921-1928), n. 1424; Beste, *Introductio in Codicem,* p. 713. Pistocchi, *De Re Beneficiali Iuxta Canones Codicis Iuris Canonici* (Taurini: Marietti, 1928), 416 ff., holds that it is an obligation binding in justice.

by his own industry, most of which are derived indirectly from the office though not from the endowment itself; *bona beneficialia*, i. e. the actual capital property of the church or pious foundation, including vestments and sacred furnishings (*sacra supellex*), and the income derived from that actual capital property; *bona parsimonialia*, i. e. that portion of an income which an ordinary incumbent would have spent for his sustenance but which the present incumbent has saved by living frugally.

An incumbent is free to make whatever disposition he may desire of the *bona patrimonalia, quasi-patrimonialia* and *parsimonialia*, since these are funds over which he has complete dominion. The ordinary incumbent of a benefice, however, is not permitted the free disposition of the *bona beneficialia*, since he has not complete dominion over these. He may make use of the furnishings as well as that portion of the income that is necessary for his fitting sustenance, but he is not free to dispose of the capital assets or indeed of any surplus of the income as he likes. The law obliges him to give such surplus either to poor persons or to charitable institutions.[58]

[58] The free disposal of the fruits of one's benefice has ever been prohibited to clerics by the law of the Church. Cf. cc. 1, 5, X, *de peculio clericorum*, III, 25; c. 12, X, *de testamentis et ultimis voluntatibus*, III, 26; cc. 1, 2, *de successionibus ad intestato*, III, 27. Alexander III and the Third Lateran Council condemned the custom that had sprung up of making such dispositions. Cf. cc. 7-9, X, *de testamentis et ultimis voluntatibus*, III, 26. From the fourteenth century such property escheated at the death of the incumbent to the Apostolic Camera (*spoliorum camera*). Custom, however, soon derogated this law. Moreover, special privileges were given to clerics living in and near Rome to dispose of the fruits of their benefice freely, "*vel superstites vel appetente morte.*" Cf. Sixtus IV, const. "*Etsi universis*," I ian. 1474—*Bull. Rom.* V, 211. When Pius IV (1559-1565) declared that the estate of a cleric derived from profits of trade was to go to the Apostolic Camera at the cleric's death, he expressly excepted these privileged Roman clerics. Cf. const. "*Romanus Pontifex*," 5 nov. 1560—*Bull. Rom.*, VII, 789. It was the mind of the Council of Trent that the only disposal of the income of one's benefice that could be tolerated was to the poor. Cf. sess. XXV, *de ref.*, cc. 1, 9. Canon 1473 enunciates the present law in this regard. For a more complete treatment of the historical sources of this law, one may with profit consult the copious notes to be found in Hannan, *The Canon Law of Wills*, The Catholic University of America Canon Law Studies, n. 86 (Washington, D. C.: The Catholic University of America, 1934), nn. 251-284.

Besides the free disposal of the *bona patrimonialia, quasi-patrimonialia* and *parsimonialia*, cardinals who are incumbents of benefices are also free by privilege to dispose of certain of the *bona beneficialia.* They are permitted to dispose of the revenues of their benefices, either by donation inter vivos or by last will and testament to whomsoever they desire.[59] For a cardinal who has a domicile in Rome, this privilege in a modified form is extended to the *sacra supellex* of their chapels. Such a cardinal may donate or will these to any church, public oratory, pious institution or to any ecclesiastical person, moral or physical; the transaction to be effective upon the death of the cardinal. In using this privilege, Cardinals are exhorted to give preference to their title churches and other churches that they have administered or held *in commendam.* Should a Roman cardinal fail to make use of this privilege, then, with the exception of his rings and pectoral crosses, upon the cardinal's death all the sacred furnishings of his chapel escheat to the Papal Sacristy.[60]

If a cardinal is a residential bishop of any diocese other than the suburbicarian diocese, the *sacra supellex* of his chapel, with the exception of rings and pectoral crosses,[61] automatically upon the cardinal's demise become the property of the Cathedral Church. An exception is also made for those sacred furnishings that such a cardinal has purchased with his own personal funds. In this case, however, legitimate proof of the fact must be given.[62]

These privileges granted to cardinals in canon 239, § 1, n. 19 and in canon 1298, have a long and varied history. Until the middle of the sixteenth century, cardinals like all other clerics, were not permitted the free disposition of the fruits or income of their benefices. Thomassinus (1619-1695) reported that it was Paul III (1534-1549) who first granted cardinals the faculty of freely disposing of goods acquired from their benefices, even by last will.[63]

[59] Canon 239, § 1, n. 19.

[60] Canon 1298.

[61] Should a pectoral cross of any residential bishop contain a relic of the True Cross, this relic is to be transmitted to his successor. Cf. canon 1299, § 1, together with canon 1288.

[62] Canon 1299, § 1.

[63] *Vetus et nova ecclesiae disciplina circa beneficia et beneficiarios* (3 tom.

Julius III (1550-1555), who succeeded Paul III, definitely made mention of the fact that cardinals enjoyed such a privilege, which, he decreed, did not extend to the *fructus inexactos* of their benefices, i. e. debts that were owed to a cardinal-incumbent of a benefice, which debts he had failed to collect before his death. Such goods, upon the cardinal's death, were to become the property of his successor in the benefice in those regions where there were no collectors for the *Spoliorum Camera*. Moreover, Julius reaffirmed a decree of a predecessor, Clement VII (1523-1534), by declaring that no cardinal had the faculty to dispose of the ornaments and sacred furnishings (*sacra supellex*) which he made use of in his private chapel or in papal functions. These escheated upon a cardinal's demise to the Papal Sacristy.[64]

Pius V (1566-1572), led to do so by the scandalous abuse of

in 10 vols., Magontiaci, 1787), VII, tom. III, lib. II, cap. XLVIII, n. 10 (henceforth cited simply as Thomassinus). Although this so-called *"bulla Compacti"* of Paul III was unavailable to the writer, it seems certain that cardinals did not enjoy such a faculty prior to the time of Paul III. This conclusion is substantiated by the fact that Hieronymus Albanus (1504-1591), whose work, *Liber de Cardinalatu* was published in 1541, did not mention this faculty among the many privileges he included as enjoyed by cardinals at that time. It was mentioned by Anastasius Germonius (1551-1627), who lived just after Paul III as a contemporary of Albanus, in his work *Tractatus de Indultis Apostolicis* which was published in 1591. In view of these facts, it may be concluded that this faculty was granted to cardinals by Paul III, for his successor, Julius III (1550-1555), made mention of it as a faculty already possessed by the cardinals.

[64] Motu propr. *"Cum sicut nobis,"* 26 iun. 1550—*Fontes*, n. 84. Regarding the sacred furnishings of cardinals' chapels the pontiff declared: *"Huiusmodi paramenta ac ornamenta Cappellae ipsorum Cardinalium quae iam tanto tempore, quod eius initii hominum memoria non habetur, Cappellae Apostolicae in qua Missae Papales celebrantur devolvi consueverunt."* This entire decree was directed against the heirs of cardinals, who often attempted even by the threat of lawsuits to obtain not only more than they were actually willed by the deceased cardinal, but even more than the cardinal was permitted to dispose of in his will. Nepotism, which plagued this period of Church history, was often the occasion of a cardinal abusing his faculty by disposing of certain goods to which the faculty did not extend. The majority of decrees issued on these matters from the time of Julius III to that of Innocent XII (1691-1700) were occasioned by the inroads of nepotism.

privileges that nepotism was occasioning, firmly decreed that the sacred furnishings of churches and other benefices were the property of said places and could not be disposed of by anyone regardless of any faculty he might have of disposing of the fruits of his benefice.[65]

Despite the decree of Julius III, the custom sprung up for a newly promoted cardinal to seek from the pontiff who had appointed him, four indults, two of which were the following: (1) an indult containing the faculty to dispose of the income of his benefices by last will to whomsoever he desired; (2) an indult permitting him to will the sacred furnishings that he made use of in his private chapel and at papal functions to whomsoever he desired. This latter faculty had been excluded by Julius III. These indults were freely granted by the pontiffs when asked for by a cardinal. If a cardinal failed to seek these indults he had no freedom whatsoever to dispose of his income or *sacra supellex.*[66]

Urban VIII (1623-1644), admitting that he himself had freely granted cardinals the indult of disposing of the sacred furnishings used by them in their chapels and at papal functions, confirmed and re-established in practice the decrees of his predecessors Clement VII and Julius III by declaring that regardless of any indults, these goods upon the death of a cardinal were to become the property of the Papal Sacristy.[67] Clement IX (1667-1669) extended the cardinalitial indult of disposing of the fruits of their benefices to include the *"fructos inconsumptos, quae antehac nullo modo disponere poterant."*[68]

Innocent XII (1691-1700) because of the abusive practices that nepotism was still fostering, decreed that all special indults that had been granted to certain cardinals permitting them to dispose of

[65] Const. *"Romani Pontifices,"* 30 aug. 1567—*Fontes,* n. 123.

[66] Cf. Plati, *De Dignitate et Officio Cardinalis,* 407, n. 82; 416, n. 134; 418, nn. 136-137. Cf. also Hannan, *op. cit.,* n. 319. It is to be noted that the *sacra supellex* pertaining to any benefices that a cardinal held could not be disposed of. Upon his death these furnishings became the property of his successor. Even today, the sacred furnishings of a cardinal who is a residential bishop, escheat, with a few exceptions, to his cathedral church (canon 1299).

[67] Const. *"Aequum est,"* 19 iul. 1642—*Fontes,* n. 225.

[68] Motu propr. *"Cum a prima,"* 28 feb. 1668—*Fontes,* n. 242.

ecclesiastical goods over which they had no dominion, were to be considered reduced to the usual terms of the indults granted to all cardinals in this regard, i. e. to dispose of the income of their benefices with the added extension permitted by Clement IX, whose decree Innocent confirmed.[69]

Once again, despite the latest decree of Urban VIII mentioned above, it became customary for the pontiffs to concede indults to the cardinals permitting them to dispose of the sacred furnishings used by them in their private chapels and in papal functions, *but only on the condition that such bequests be made to churches, public chapels or pious institutions.* Benedict XIV (1740-1758) confirmed this practice adding that whenever he granted such indults to cardinals he exhorted them that in making such bequests they consider firstly those churches with which they were connected.[70]

Finally, Pius IX (1846-1878) declared that all the sacred furnishings used by a cardinal of the Roman Curia, *unless he had obtained the faculty of disposing of them,* regardless of their value were to escheat to the Papal Chapel at the cardinal's death. If a cardinal was a bishop of a diocese other than a suburbicarian diocese, these objects at his death were to become the property of the cathedral church.[71]

The Code accords cardinals the faculties of disposing of the surplus income from their benefices to whomsoever they desire, even by last will, and, provided they are not also diocesan bishops, of disposing of their sacred furnishings either by donation *inter vivos* or by last will to any ecclesiastical person, physical or moral.[72] Prior

[69] Const. *"Ut iudicium,"* 15 oct. 1693—*Fontes,* n. 256.

[70] Const. *"Inter Arduas,"* 22 apr. 1749—*Fontes,* n. 396.

[71] Litt. ap. *"Quum illud,"* 1 iun. 1847—*Fontes,* n. 505. He expressly mentioned the articles subject to this decree as mitres, chasubles, copes, tunics, dalmatics, gloves, albs, cinctures, linen amices and the like; chalices, patens, pyxes, ostensoria, thuribles, the holy water vessel with aspersorium, the pitcher and basin, holy oil vessels, cruets and basin, the bell, candelabra, the cross, croziers and the faldstool. The pectoral cross and ring are excepted. Cf. Berutti, *Institutiones Iuris Canonici,* IV (Taurini-Romae: Marietti, 1940), n. 90.

[72] Canons 1473, 239, § 1, n. 19, 1298.

to the Code the individual cardinals were obliged to seek these faculties by way of indult from the Roman Pontiff.[73]

Throughout the preceding historical summary of the legislation on this matter it was necessary to speak of cardinals as holding more than one benefice. Although the general law of the Church has always forbidden a plurality of benefices, history shows that dispensations from this law were often granted. This was especially true in the case of a residential bishop who was promoted to the cardinalate being permitted to hold both his episcopal see and his cardinalitial benefice. Paul III sought the counsel of his cardinals in this matter and they claimed that the cardinalitial and episcopal benefices seemed to be incompatible because of the law of residence attached to each. In view of the fact that the law did not permit an individual to hold two incompatible offices, the Pope granted dispensations for such cardinals.[74]

Pope Sixtus V (1585-1590) declared that upon promotion to the cardinalate a cleric automatically forfeited all churches and every other type of benefice he held, unless a special concession was made for their retention. However, since the benefices of Patriarchates, Archbishoprics, Bishoprics and those of Abbots are not incompatible with the cardinalate, Sixtus declared that the retention of such benefices was to be considered as automatically conceded when the incumbent was promoted to the cardinalate. All other benefices that seemed to be repugnant to the cardinalitial dignity, such as those of Canons, who are bound to choir obligations in which they have a place inferior to the bishop, are to be considered incompatible, and be-

[73] Cf. Cohellius, *De Notitia Cardinalatus,* p. 172; Diana, *Resolutiones Morales,* V, Tom. 9, tract. 7, res. LXXIV, LXXXVIII, XCII; Andreucci (1684-1771), *Hierarchia Ecclesiastica,* II, diss. II, n. 33; Sipos, *Enchiridion,* p. 209, nota (19) ad calcem. Formerly cardinals sought these faculties when they were promoted, for which privilege they were obliged to contribute 600 scudi (about 3,000 lire or $600) to the Sacred Congregation for the Propagation of the Faith, in return for which they were given by the Propaganda the official ring of the cardinalate, adorned with a sapphire and with the coat-of-arms of the pontiff who promoted them engraved on its under-surface. Cf. Wernz, *Ius Decretalium,* III, n. 634; Sipos, *Enchiridion,* p. 714, Nainfa, *Costume of Prelates,* p. 141.

[74] Cf. Thomassinus, VII, Tom. II, lib. III, Cap. 5, n. 14.

come vacant *ipso facto* when the incumbent is promoted to the cardinalate unless their retention is expressly conceded.[75]

Under the present law of the Code, the cardinalate as such is considered a *consistorial, non-curata, residential benefice,* known in the old law as a major benefice.[76] It has already been shown that the cardinalate as such is an office in the strict sense of canon 145.[77] That it is also a benefice is apparent from the fact that it fulfills all the conditions required for a benefice by canon 1409.[78] The revenues annexed to it are the following. From the time of Paul II (1464-1471) all cardinals residing in Rome have the right to a minimum competence of at least 4,000 scudi (about 20,000 Lire or $4,000) a year. This is paid to them monthly by the Holy See and is known as the *piatto cardinalizio.*[79] To the above named sum are added the proceeds from the *massa communis,* a common fund of the College of Cardinals, created by revenues from real estate and consistorial fees. This fund is administered by the Chamberlin (*Camerarius*) of the College of Cardinals, who pays annually to the cardinals residing at the Roman Curia sums equal to from $250 to $300. This is known as the *Rotulus Cardinalitius.* Finally, these cardinals receive about $100 annually from the papal funds to cover indemnification for postage.[80]

In virtue of this benefice, all cardinals are obliged to reside at

[75] Const. *"Sanctissimus,"* 16 mar. 1588—*Fontes,* n. 163.

[76] Cf. canons 1411, n. 1, n. 5; 233; 238; Coronata, *Institutiones,* II, 362; Cappello, *Summa Iuris Canonici,* II (Romae: Universitas Gregoriana, 1930), 472, n. 863; Sipos, *Enchiridion,* p. 766; Beste, *Introductio in Codicem,* p. 698; Haydt, *Reserved Benefices,* pp. 86-87.

[77] Cf. *above,* p. 40.

[78] Beneficium ecclesiasticum est ens iuridicum a competente ecclesiastica auctoritate in perpetuum constitutum seu erectum, constans officio sacro et iure percipiendi reditus ex dote officio adnexos. The various modes of supporting a benefice are enumerated in canon 1410.

[79] However, any revenues which a cardinal may draw from other benefices which he has been permitted to retain are deducted from this. Cf. Hilling, *Procedure at the Roman Curia,* p. 31.

[80] These facts are cited by Hilling, *Das Personenrecht des Codex Iuris Canonici* (Paderborn: Ferdinand Schöningh, 1924), 127-128; also in Hilling, *Procedure at the Roman Curia,* p. 31.

the Roman Curia[81] and have a right to this annual income. The cardinals who reside *in curia* receive this income as the fruits of their benefice. Cardinals, however, who are bishops of dioceses other than the suburbicarian sees, are dispensed from the law of residence *in curia,*[82] and may reside in their dioceses as residential bishops.

With reference to a cardinal holding a benefice other than his cardinalitial benefice, it is to be noted that the present law of the Code is substantially a repetition of the decree of Sixtus V mentioned above. It is stated in canon 235 that unless the Holy See grants exemptions in particular cases, not only all dignities, churches or other benefices that the new cardinal held, become vacant *ipso facto,* but also all ecclesiastical pensions are automatically forfeited by promotion to the cardinalate.[83] This canon is but an application of canon 156 which states that offices which one person cannot simultaneously administer as they should be administered are incompatible and may not be conferred on the same person.[84]

In view of this, does canon 235 apply to the case of a diocesan bishop being raised to the cardinalate? It may safely be stated that canon 235 does not apply to the case of a diocesan bishop being promoted to the cardinalate, for, since canon 235 is but a restatement of the decree promulgated by Sixtus V, it is to be interpreted, in accordance with canon 6, nn. 2, 3 in the light of Sixtus V's constitution which stated that these two offices were not incompatible.[85] Actually, the Holy See makes express provision for such cases, so that a residential bishop who is promoted to the cardinalate does not thereby forfeit his episcopal benefice.[86]

[81] Canon 238, §§ 1, 2.

[82] Canon 238, § 3.

[83] "Nisi aliter in casibus particularibus fuerit a Sancta Sede provisum, per promotionem ad sacram purpuram non solum ipso facto vacant dignitates omnes, ecclesiae, beneficia quae promotus possideat, sed etiam pensiones ecclesiasticae amittuntur."

[84] Canon 156, § 1: Nemini conferantur duo officia incompatibilia.
§ 2: Sunt incompatibilia officia quae una simul ab eodem adimpleri nequeunt.

[85] Cf. Blat, *Commentarium,* II, n. 196.

[86] Cf. Vermeersch-Creusen, *Epitome,* I, n. 349; Coronata, *Institutiones,* I, n. 322, 6; Sipos, *Enchiridion,* p. 198.

Consequently, in view of the special privilege extended to all cardinals, they may dispose of the fruits (income) that they receive from the various benefices that they have been permitted to retain after their promotion to the cardinalate, as well as from any pensions or *commendae* they have been granted after their assumption to the cardinalate.[87] This disposition they may make to anyone they wish, even by bequests in their last wills and testaments.

Article VII. Privilege of Being Buried Within a Church

Canon 1205, § 2. In ecclesiis cadavera ne sepeliantur, nisi agatur de cadaveribus Episcoporum residentialium, Abbatum vel Praelatorum *nullius* in propria ecclesia sepeliendis, vel Romani Pontificis, regalium personarum aut S.R.E. Cardinalium.

A final privilege granted to cardinals by the Code of Canon Law is that of having their mortal remains interred in a church. The principal commentary to be made on this last privilege is that before a cardinal makes known his desire to avail himself of this privilege, he should consult the civil laws of his territory, as the civil laws of many countries forbid burial within churches. In Rome itself, even cardinals are to be buried in the common city cemetery, the famous *"Campo Santo"* near the Basilica of St. Lawrence outside the Walls of the City.

[87] Cf. Coronata, *loc. cit.*

CONCLUSIONS

(1) That, of the privileges accorded to cardinals prior to the Code, some few were enjoyed as express grants of the common law, while the majority were enjoyed in virtue of the custom of the Roman Curia.

(2) That the cardinalate as such is both an office in the strict sense as well as a consistorial, residential benefice without the care of souls.

(3) That the cardinalitial privilege of using the crosier is not subject to the restrictions placed on the similar privilege of bishops by the *Caeremoniale Episcoporum.* With the exception of the four Patriarchal Basilicas of Rome, cardinals may use the crosier throughout the world without the necessity of any local Ordinary's permission.

(4) That the ordinary confessional jurisdiction which is annexed to the cardinalitial office cannot be delegated to another.

(5) That the extensive confessional jurisdiction enjoyed through privilege by cardinals does not extend to the sin of Complicity (*absolutio complicis*).

(6) Since the only reserved censures excepted from the extensive confessional jurisdiction of cardinals are those reserved *specialissimo modo* to the Holy See and those resulting from the violation of the secret of the Holy Office, the cardinalitial faculty to absolve from reserved censures extends also to those censures reserved *ab homine.*

(7) That should a cardinal in using his privilege of choosing a confessor select a priest who is under a *post sententiam* censure or excommunication or suspension, the absolutions granted by that confessor would be valid in virtue of canon 209.

(8) That the cardinalitial privilege of offering a private Mass on Holy Thursday and of celebrating successively from midnight three private Masses on Christmas, may be used by a cardinal *or* another priest at the cardinal's behest, *not by both.*

(9) That although the legislator has allowed for exceptions contained in concordats, and for legislative customs derogatory to the

privileged forum of minor clerics, no customs are tolerated against the privileged forum of cardinals.

(10) That although not expressly mentioned, cardinals are nevertheless subject to the penal decree against simony in the constitution *Vacante Sede Apostolica,* which exclusively governs papal elections.

BIBLIOGRAPHY

Sources

Acta Apostolicae Sedis, Commentarium Officiale, Romae, 1909—

Acta et Decreta Concilii Plenarii Baltimorensis Tertii, MDCCCLXXXIV, Baltimorae, 1886.

Acta Sanctae Sedis, Romae, 1865-1908.

Bouscaren, T. Lincoln, *The Canon Law Digest,* 2 vols., Milwaukee: Bruce Publishing Co., Vol. I, 1934; Vol. II, 1943.

Bullarum Diplomatum et Privilegiorum S. R. Pontificum Taurinensis Editio, 20 vols., Augustae Taurinorum, 1857-1872; 5 vols., Neapoli, 1867-1885.

Caeremoniale Episcoporum Clementis VIII, Innocentii X et Benedicti XIII, iussu editum Benedicti XIV et Leonis XIII, auctoritate recognitum, Mechliniae: H. Dessain, 1906.

Codex Iuris Canonici Pii X Pontificis Maximi iussu digestus Benedicti XV auctoritate promulgatus, Romae: Typis Polyglottis Vaticanis, 1917.

Codicis Iuris Canonici Fontes cura Emi Petri Card. Gasparri editi, Romae, postea Civitate Vaticana: Typis Polyglottis Vaticanis, 1923-1938.

Collectanea S. Congregationis de Propaganda Fide, Romae: Typographia Polyglotta, S.C. de Propaganda Fide, 1893.

Corpus Iuris Canonici, ed. Lipsiensis secunda, post Aemilii Ludovici Richteri curas instruxit Aemilius Friedberg, 2 vols., Lipsiae: Ex Officina Bernhardi Tauchnitz, 1879-1881. Editio anastatice repetita, Lipsiae, 1922.

Corpus Iuris Civilis, editio stereotypa quinta decima, 3 vols., Berolini: apud Weidmannos, 1915-1928; Vol. I: Institutiones et Digesta, 1928; Vol. II: Codex, 1915; Vol. III, Novellae, 1928.

Decreta Authentica Congregationis Sacrorum Rituum, 5 vols., Romae: Ex Typographia Polyglotta, 1898-1901. Appendix I, 1912; Appendix II, 1927.

Decreta Authentica Sacrae Congregationis Indulgentiis Sacrisque Reliquis Pareposilae, Ratisbonae, 1883.

Decretales D. Gregorii Papae IX, una cum glossis restitutae, Romae, 1582.

Decretum Gratiani Emendatum et Notationibus illustratum una cum glossis, Romae, 1582.

Hardouin, Jean, *Acta Conciliorum et Epistolae Decretales ac Constitutiones Summorum Pontificum,* 12 vols., Parisiis, 1714-1715.

Liber Sextus Decretalium D. Bonifacii Papae VIII, una cum Clementinis et Extravagentibus tem D. Joannis XXII tum Communibus, una cum earum glossis, Romae, 1582.

Mansi, J. D., *Sacrorum Conciliorum Nova et Amplissima Collectio,* 53 vols. in 59, Parisiis, 1901-1927.

Missale Romanum ex decreto Sacrosancti Concilii Tridentini restitutum S. Pii V Pontificis Maximi jussu editum aliorum pontificum cura recognitum a Pio X reformatum et Benedicti XV auctoritate vulgatum, editio XIV iuxta Typicam Vaticanam, Ratisbonae: sumptibus et typis Friderici Pustet, 1930.

Potthast, A., *Regesta Pontificum Romanorum inde ab A. post Christum natum 1198 ad A. 1304,* 2 vols., Berolini, 1874-1875.

Rituale Romanum Pauli V Pontificis Maximi iussu editum aliorumque Pontificum cura recognitum atque auctoritate SSmi D.N. Pii Papae XI ad normam Codicis Iuris Canonici accomodatum, editio iuxta typicam vaticanam, Mechliniae: H. Dessain, 1929.

Schroeder, H. J., *Canons and Decrees of the Council of Trent,* original text with English translation, St. Louis: Herder, 1941.

———, *Disciplinary Decrees of the General Councils,* St. Louis: Herder, 1937.

Reference Works

Albanus, Ioannes Hieronymus, Card., *Liber De Cardinalatu,* Romae, 1541.

Albitius (Albizzi), Franciscus, Card., *Disceptatio de Iurisdictione quam habent S.R.E. Cardinales in Ecclesiis Titulorum*—contained in De Luca, *Theatrum Veritatis et Iustitiae* (15 tom. in 9 vols., Coloniae-Agrippinae, 1706), IV, tom. VIII, 220 sq.

Andreucci, Andreas, *Hierarchia Ecclesiastica,* 2 vols., Romae, 1766.

Augustine, Charles, *A Commentary on the New Code of Canon Law,* 8 vols., St. Louis: Herder; Vol. II: *Clergy and Hierarchy,* 3. ed., 1919; Vol. VI: *Administrative Law,* 3. ed., 1931.

Ayrinhac, H. A., *Penal Legislation in the New Code of Canon Law,* revised by P. J. Lydon, New York: Benziger, 1936.

Azorius, J., *Institutiones Morales,* 3 vols.; Vol. II, Mediolani, 1617.

Baart, Peter A., *The Roman Court,* Milwaukee, 1895.

Barbosa, Agostino, *Iuris ecclesiastici universi libri III,* 3 vols., Lugduni, 1650.

Barrett, John, *A Comparative Study of the Councils of Baltimore and the Code of Canon Law,* The Catholic University of America Canon Law Studies, n. 83, Washington, D. C.: The Catholic University of America, 1932.

Barry, Garrett, *Violation of the Cloister,* The Catholic University of America Canon Law Studies, n. 148, Washington, D. C.: The Catholic University of America Press, 1942.

Belardo, M., *De Iuribus S.R.E. Cardinalium in Titulis,* Romae: Anonim. Libr. Cattolica Italiana, 1939.

Bellarminus, Robertus, Card., *De Controversiis Christianae Fidei adversus huius temporis Haereticos,* 3 vols. in 2, ed. cura Card. Sforza, Neapoli, 1856-1858.

Benko, Matthew, *The Abbot Nullius,* The Catholic University of America Canon Law Studies, n. 173, Washington, D. C.: The Catholic University of America Press, 1943.

Berutti, Christophorus, *Institutiones Iuris Canonici,* Vol. IV, Taurini-Romae: Marietti, 1940.

Beste, *Introductio in Codicem,* Collegeville, Minn.: St. John's Abbey Press, 1938.

Blat, A., *Commentarium Textus Codicis Iuris Canonici,* 5 vols. in 7, Romae: Apud Angelicum, 1921-1938; Vol. II, 1921; Vol. III, Pars I, 2. ed., 1924; Vol. III, Pars I, 3. ed., 1938.

Bliley, Nicholas, *Altars According to the Code of Canon Law,* The Catholic University of America Canon Law Studies, n. 38, Washington, D. C.: The Catholic University of America, 1927.

Burke, Thomas J., *Competence in Ecclesiastical Tribunals,* The Catholic University of America Canon Law Studies, n. 14, Washington, D. C.: The Catholic University of America, 1922.

Cappello, Felix M., *Summa Iuris Canonici,* Vol. II, Romae: Universitas Gregoriana, 1930.

———, *Summa Iuris Publici Ecclesiastici,* 4. ed., Romae: Universitas Gregoriana, 1936.

———, *Tractatus Canonico-Moralis de Censuris,* Taurinorum Augustae: Marietti, 1925.

———, *Tractatus Canonico-Moralis de Sacramentis,* 3 vols. in 6; Vol. II, Pars I: *De Poenitentia,* Romae: Marietti, 1928; Vol. II, Pars III: *De Sacra Ordinatione,* Romae: Marietti, 1935.

Cicognani, Amleto, *Canon Law,* authorized English version, by J. O'Hara and F. Brennan, Philadelphia: Dolphin Press, 1935.

Cipollini, Albertus, *De Censuris Latae Sententiae iuxta Codicem Iuris Canonici,* Taurini: Marietti, 1925.

Cocchi, Guidus, *Commentarium in Codicem Iuris Canonici,* 5 vols. in 8, Taurinorum Augustae, 1932-1940; Vol. I, 5. ed. recognita, 1938; Vol. III, ed. 4. recognita, 1938; Vol. V, 4. ed., 1938.

Cohellius, Jacobus, *Notitia Cardinalatus,* Romae, 1653.

Coleman, John J., *The Minister of Confirmation,* The Catholic University of America Canon Law Studies, n. 125, Washington, D. C.: The Catholic University of America Press, 1941.

Connors, Charles P., *Extra-Judicial Procurators in the Code of Canon Law,* The Catholic University of America Canon Law Studies, n. 190, Washington, D. C.: The Catholic University of America Press, 1944.

Coronata, Mattheus Conte a, *Institutiones Iuris Canonici,* 5 vols., Taurini: Marietti, 1928-1936; Vol. I, 1928; Vol. II, 1928; Vol. II, 1933; Vol. IV, 1935.

———, *De Locis et Temporibus Sacris,* Augustae Taurinorum: Marietti, 1922.

Creusen, J., *Religious Men and Women in the Code*, translated from the French by E. F. Garesche, S.J.; fourth English edition revised and edited to conform with the fifth French edition by Adam C. Ellis, S.J., Milwaukee: Bruce, 1942.

D'Annibale, Josephus, Card., *Summula Theologiae Moralis*, 5. ed., 3 vols., Romae, 1908.

De Luca, Ioannes Baptista, Card., *Theatrum Veritatis et Iustitiae*, 15 toms. in 9 vols., Coloniae-Agrippinae, 1706.

De Meester, A., *Iuris Canonici et Iuris Canonico-Civilis Compendium*, 4 vols., Brugis, 1921-1928.

De Sobradillo, Agapito, *De Religiosarum Confessariis*, Torino: R. Berutti Co., 1932.

Diana, Antoninus, *Resolutiones Morales, ed. novissima*, 10 toms. in 5 vols., Venetiis, 1728.

Diekamp, F., *Theologiae Dogmaticae Manuale*, 2 vols., 6. ed., Parisiis: Desclée et Socii, 1934.

Downs, John E., *The Concept of Clerical Immunity*, The Catholic University of America Canon Law Studies, n. 126, Washington, D. C.: The Catholic University of America Press, 1941.

Dugan, Henry F., *The Judiciary Department of the Diocesan Curia*, The Catholic University of America Canon Law Studies, n. 26, Washington, D. C.: The Catholic University of America, 1925.

Fagnanus, Prosper, *Commentaria in Quinque Libros Decretalium*, 5 vols. in 3, Venetiis, 1696.

Fanfani, Ludovicus, *De Indulgentiis*, 2. ed., notabiliter aucta, Romae, 1926.

Feldhaus, Aloysius, *Oratories* The Catholic University of America Canon Law Studies n. 42, Washington, D. C.: The Catholic University of America, 1927.

Ferraris, Lucius, *Prompta Bibliotheca, Canonica, Juridica, Moralis, Theologica, necnon Ascetica, Polemica, Rubricistica, Historica*, ed. Migne, 8 vols., Parisiis, 1860-1863.

Gattico, *De Usu Altaris Portatilis*, Romae, 1746.

Gasparri, Petrus, *De Sanctissima Eucharistia*, 2 vols., Parisiis et Lugduni, 1897.

Germonius, Anastasius, *De Sacrorum Immunitatibus Libri Tres*, Romae, 1591.

———, *Tractatus de Indultis Apostolicis*, Romae, 1590.

Gomez, *Commentaria in Regulas Cancellariae Iudiciales*, Lugduni, 1543.

Görres-Gesselschaft zur Wissenschaft im katholischen Deutschland, Köln, 1876-1908, Paderborn, 1909-1937; *Sektion für Rechts und Staatswissenschaft*, Köln, 1908, Paderborn, 1909-1937.

Hagedorn, Francis E., *General Legislation on Indulgences*, The Catholic University of America Canon Law Studies, n. 22, Washington, D. C.: The Catholic University of America, 1924.

Hannan, Jerome D., *The Canon Law of Wills*, The Catholic University of America Canon Law Studies, n. 86, Washington, D. C.: The Catholic University of America, 1934.

Haydt, John, *Reserved Benefices,* The Catholic University of America Canon Law Studies, n. 161, Washington, D. C.: The Catholic University of America Press, 1942.

Hilling, Nicolaus, *Das Personenrecht des Codex Iuris Canonici,* Paderborn: Ferdinand Schöningh, 1924.

———, *Procedure at the Roman Curia,* translated from the German, New York, 1907.

Hinschius, Paul, *Das Kirchenrecht der Katholiken und Protestanten in Deutschland,* 6 vols., Berlin, 1869-1897; Vols. I-IV: *System des katholischen Kirchenrechts,* Berlin, 1869-1888.

Hostiensis, Card. (Henricus de Segusio), *Commentaria in Quinque Libros Decretalium,* 6 vols. in 3, Venetiis, 1581.

Kearney, Raymond A., *The Principles of Delegation,* The Catholic University of America Canon Law Studies, n. 55, Washington, D. C.: The Catholic University of America, 1929.

Król, John J., *The Defendant in Contentious Trials,* The Catholic University of America Canon Law Studies, n. 146, Washington, D. C.: The Catholic University of America Press, 1942.

Laymann, Paulus, *Theologia Moralis,* ed. nova, Venetiis, 1630.

Lega, Michael, *Praelectiones in Textum Iuris Canonici, De Delictis et Poenis,* 2. ed., Romae, 1910.

Lehmkuhl, Augustinus, *Theologia Moralis,* 2 vols., 10. ed., Friburgi Brisgoviae, 1902.

Linahen, Leo J., *De Absolutione Complicis in Peccato Turpi,* The Catholic University of America Canon Law Studies, n. 164, Washington, D. C.: The Catholic University of America Press, 1942.

Manfredus, Hieronymus, *De Perfecto Cardinali S.R.E. Liber,* Bononiae, 1584.

Maroto, Philippus, *Institutiones Iuris Canonici,* 2 vols., Romae, Matriti, 1919-1921; Vol. I, ed. 3a, Romae, 1921; Vol. II, Matriti, 1919.

McCormick, Robert E., *Confessors of Religious,* The Catholic University of America Canon Law Studies, n. 33, Washington, D. C.: The Catholic University of America, 1926.

Mörsdorf, Klaus, *Die Rechtssprache des Codex Juris Canonici — Görres-Gesellschaft zur Pflege der Wissenschaft im katholischen Deutschland; Sektion für Rechts und Staatswissenschaft,* Köln, 1908, Paderborn, 1909-1937, Vol. 74, Paderborn; Verlag Ferdinand Schöningh, 1937.

Nainfa, John A., *Costume of Prelates of the Catholic Church,* Baltimorae: John Murphy Co., 1926.

O'Connell, J., *The Celebration of Mass,* 3 vols., Milwaukee: Bruce Publishing Co., 1940-1941.

Ottenthal, E., *Regulae Cancellariae Apostolicae, Die Päpstlichen Kanzleiregeln von Johannes XXII bis Nicolaus V,* Innsbruck, 1888.

Paschang, John L., *The Sacramentals According to the Code of Canon Law*, The Catholic University of America Canon Law Studies, n. 28, Washington, D. C.: The Catholic University of America, 1925.

Pernicone, Joseph M., *The Ecclesiastical Prohibition of Books*, The Catholic University of America Canon Law Studies, n. 72, Washington, D. C.: The Catholic University of America, 1932.

Petra, Vincentius, Card., *Commentaria ad Constitutiones Apostolicas*, 5 tom. in 2 vols., Venetiis, 1729.

Pistocchi, M., *De Re Beneficiali iuxta Canones Codicis Iuris Canonici*, Taurini: Marietti, 1928.

Plati (Piatti), Girolamo, Card., *De Dignitate Et Officio Cardinalis*, 6. ed., cura Alexandri Card. Spada, Romae, 1836.

Reiffenstuel, Anacletus, *Ius Canonicum Universum*, 6 vols., Romae, 1831-1834.

Riganti, *Commentaria in Regulas, Constitutiones et Ordinationes Cancellariae Apostolicae*, 4 vols. in 2, Coloniae Allobrogum, 1751.

Roelker, Edward G., *Principles of Privilege According to the Code of Canon Law*, The Catholic University of America Canon Law Studies, n. 35, Washington, D. C.: The Catholic University of America, 1926.

Ryder, Raymond A., *Simony*, The Catholic University of America Canon Law Studies, n. 65, Washington, D. C.: The Catholic University of America, 1931.

Sägmüller, Johannes B., *Die Thätigkeit und Stellung der Cardinäle bis Papst Bonifaz VIII*, Freiburg, 1896.

———, *Lehrbuch des katholischen Kirchenrechts*, Vol. I, Freiburg im Bresgau: Herder, 1925-1934.

Sanchez, Thomas, *Consilia Moralia*, 2 vols. in 1, Lugduni, 1634.

Schaaf, Valentine T., *The Cloister*, The Catholic University of America Canon Law Studies, n. 13, Washington, D. C.: The Catholic University of America, 1921.

Schmalzgrueber, Franciscus, *Ius Ecclesiasticum Universum*, 5 vols. in 12, Romae, 1843-1845.

Sipos, Stephanus, *Enchiridion Iuris Canonici*, 3. ed., Pecs Hungary: Haladás, R. T., 1936.

Sole, Jacobus, *Praelectiones in Liber V Codicis Iuris Canonici, De Delictis et Poenis*, Romae: Pustet, 1920.

Stadalnikas, Casimir, *Reservation of Censures*, The Catholic University of America Canon Law Studies, n. 208, Washington, D. C.: The Catholic University of America Press, 1944.

Suarez, Franciscus, *Opera Omnia*, 26 vols., Parisiis, 1856-1861.

Thomassinus, L., *Vetus et nova ecclesiae disciplina circa beneficia et beneficiarios*, 3 tom. in 10 vols., Magontiaci, 1787.

Toso, Albertus, *Ad Codicem Iuris Canonici Commentaria Minora*, 5 vols., 1920-1934; Vol. II, Tom. I, Romae, 1922; Vol. II, Tom. II, Romae, 1923.

Tuscus (Tosco, Toschi), Domenico, Card., *Practicae Conclusiones Iuris in omni foro Frequentiores*, 9 vols., Lugduni, 1634-1670.

Van Hove, A., *Prolegomena ad Codicem Iuris Canonici, Commentarium Lovaniense*, Vol. I, tom. I, Mechliniae et Romae: Dessain, 1928.

Vermeersch, A.-Creusen, J., *Epitome Iuris Canonici*, 3 vols., Mechliniae, Romae: H. Dessain, Vol. I, 6. ed., 1937; Vol. II, ed. 5a., 1934; Vol. III, ed. 5a., 1936.

Vromant, G., *Ius Missionariorum*, Vol. VI: *De Bonis Temporalibus Ecclesiae*, Louvain, 1927.

Wernz, Franciscus X., *Ius Decretalium ad Usum Praelectionum in Scholis Textus Canonici sive Iuris Decretalium*, 6 vols. in 7, Romae-Prati, 1899-1913.

Woywod, Stanislaus, *A Practical Commentary on the Code of Canon Law*, revised by Rev. Callistus Smith, 2 vols., New York: Joseph F. Wagner, 1943.

Ziolkowski, Thaddeus S., *The Consecration and Blessing of Churches*, The Catholic University of America Canon Law Studies, n. 187, Washington, D. C.: The Catholic University of America Press, 1943.

Periodicals

American Ecclesiastical Review, The, Philadelphia, 1889-1944; Washington, D. C., 1944—

Analecta Iuris Pontificii, Romae, 1855-1869; Parisiis, 1872-1891.

Apollinaris, Romae, 1928—.

Archiv für katholisches Kirchenrecht, Innsbruck, 1857-1861; Mainz, 1862—

Clergy Review, The, London, 1931—

Commentarium pro Religiosis, Romae, 1920-1934.

Commentarium pro Religiosis et Missionariis, Romae, 1935—

Historisches Jahrbuch, Im Auftrage der Görres-Gesellschaft, Munster, 1880-1882; Munchen, 1883-1919.

Homiletic and Pastoral Review, The, New York, 1900—

Jurist, The, Washington, D. C., 1941—

Jus Pontificium, Romae, 1921—

Monitore Ecclesiastico, Il, Romae, 1876—

Periodica de Re Canonica et Morali, Brugia, 1905—; ab anno, 1927: *Periodica de Re Canonica, Morali, Liturgica.*

Razon y Fe, Madrid, 1901—

Studia Et Documenta Historiae Et Iuris, Romae, 1935—

Zeitschrift für öffenliches Recht, Wien und Berlin, 1919/1920—

PRINCIPAL ARTICLES

Ayrinhac, H. A., "The Motu Proprio 'Quantavis Diligentia'"—*AER*, XLVII (1912), 303-315.

Baumgarten, P. M., "Die Ubersendung des roten Hutes"—*HJ*, XXV (1905), 99.

Christ, J., "The Origin and Development of the Term 'Title'"—*Jurist*, IV (1944), 101-123.

"Dignité des Cardinauz"—*AIP*, II (1857), 1908.

Gomez, M., "De Regularum Confessionibus"—*CpR*, VIII (1927), 359-374.

Kuttner, Stephan, "Die Konstitutionen des ersten allgemeinen Konzils von Lyon"—*Studia Et Documenta Historiae Et Iuris*, VI (1940), 120-124.

Maroto, Philippus, "Commentarium in Responsum P.C.I. ad Can. 239, § 1, nn. 12, 13, 24"—*Apollinaris*, VIII (1935), 51-54.

Köstler, R., "Der Aufbau des katholischen Kirchenrechts. Ein Beitrag zur theorie seiner Quellen"—*ZFOR*, Bd. VI (Springer, 1922), 479.

Sajó, L., "Der Purpur des Fürst-Primas von Ungarn"—*AKKR*, LXVII (1892), 433.

Vermeersch, A., "De Clausura Monialium"—*Periodica*, XIX (1930), 12*-15*.

ABBREVIATIONS

AAS—*Acta Apostolicae Sedis.*
AER—*The American Ecclesiastical Review.*
AIP—*Analecta Iuris Pontificii.*
AKKR—*Archiv für katholisches Kirchenrecht.*
ASS—*Acta Sanctae Sedis.*
CpR—*Commentarium pro Religiosis.*
PCI—Pontificia Commissio ad Codicis Canones authentice Interpretandos.
HJ—*Historisches Jahrbuch.*
Fontes—*Codicis Iuris Canonici Fontes.*
S. C. C.—Sacra Congregatio Concilii.
S. C. de Prop. Fide—Sacra Congregatio de Propaganda Fide.
S. C. S. Off.—Suprema Congregatio Sancti Officii.
S. R. C.—Sacrorum Rituum Congregatio.
ZFOR—*Zeitschrift für öffenliches Recht.*

ALPHABETICAL INDEX

BIOGRAPHICAL NOTE

Harry Gerard Hynes was born on October 25, 1917, in Chester, Pennsylvania. After completing his grammar school education in St. Michael's and St. Robert's Schools in the same city, he entered St. Robert's High School of Chester. In September, 1932, he entered the Seminary of St. Charles of Borromeo, Overbrook, Pennsylvania, where he pursued his preparatory and philosophical studies. In the summer of 1938 he was appointed to the North American College, Rome, Italy, for the pursuance of his theological studies. In May, 1940, he received the degree of Bachelor of Sacred Theology from the Pontifical Gregorian University in Rome. With Italy's entrance into World War II the North American College was closed. He returned to this country to complete his studies at the Theological College of the Catholic University of America. In May, 1942, he received the Licentiate in Sacred Theology and was ordained to the priesthood in Philadelphia on May 30, 1942. In September of that year he was appointed to take graduate studies in Canon Law at the Catholic University of America, from which he received in May, 1943, the degree of Bachelor of Canon Law, and in May, 1944, the degree of Licentiate in Canon Law.

www.ingramcontent.com/pod-product-compliance
Lightning Source LLC
LaVergne TN
LVHW050231080826
844660LV00012B/513

* 9 7 8 0 8 1 3 2 2 4 0 1 5 *